VERSAILLES
A Private Invitation

VERSAILLES
A Private Invitation

Foreword by CATHERINE PÉGARD

Introduction by LAURENT SALOMÉ

Text by GUILLAUME PICON

Photography by FRANCIS HAMMOND

Flammarion

CHÂTEAU DE VERSAILLES

Executive Editor
Suzanne Tise-Isoré
Style & Design Collection

Editorial Coordination
Sarah Rozelle
Pauline Garrone

Graphic Design
Bernard Lagacé
Lysandre Le Cléac'h

Public Establishment of the Château, Museum, and National Estate of Versailles
Denis Verdier-Magneau, *Director of Cultural Development*

Jean-Vincent Bacquart, *Head of Publishing Services*
assisted by Cécile Bouchayer *and* Yves Carlier

Translated from the French by
David Radzinowicz
Deke Dusinberre

Copyediting and Proofreading
Helen Woodhall
Lindsay Porter

Production
Corinne Trovarelli

Color Separation
Arciel Graphic, Paris

Printed by
Stamperia Artistica Nazionale, Torino

Simultaneously published in French as
Versailles: Invitation privée

Flammarion S.A.
87, quai Panhard et Levassor
75647 Paris Cedex 13
editions.flammarion.com
styleetdesign-flammarion.com

17 18 19 3 2 1
ISBN: 978-2-08-020337-3
Edition Number: L.01EBTN000804
Legal Deposit: 10/2017

PAGE 2
Named for its white-and-gold wood paneling, the Geography Room, formerly the Gold Room
links the King's Private Apartments with the Apollo Room in the *grand appartement*. After 1755,
it was used to store the king's hairpieces and became known as the Cabinet of the Wigs.

PAGE 6
Head of Apollo or the Sun (detail on the Royal Gate). Louis XIV chose the Sun
as his emblem on the occasion of the Carrousel of 1662.

PAGE 7
Executed around 1680 under the direction of Jules Hardouin-Mansart, first architect
to the king, the Royal Gate cordoned the main courtyard off from the Royal Court.
It was partially dismantled under Louis XV during the construction of the Gabriel Wing
and then melted down during the Revolution. Lasting two years, its restoration necessitated
some 15 tons of iron and 100,000 pieces of goldleaf. It was re-erected in 2008.

CONTENTS

II   *Foreword by* CATHERINE PÉGARD

15   *Introduction by* LAURENT SALOMÉ

18   THE CHÂTEAU DE VERSAILLES

24   THE STAIRCASES OF VERSAILLES

35   THE KING'S SUITE

53   THE QUEEN'S SUITE

60   THE ROYAL CHAPEL

78   THE KING'S APARTMENT

90   THE KING'S PRIVATE APARTMENT

124   MARIE-ANTOINETTE'S PRIVATE ROOMS

148   THE QUEEN'S PRIVATE APARTMENT

156   THE APARTMENTS OF THE ROYAL MISTRESSES

166   THE APARTMENTS OF THE DAUPHIN AND DAUPHINE

176   THE HISTORY GALLERIES

198   THE ROYAL OPERA

214   THE STABLES

223   THE GARDENS OF THE CHÂTEAU

240   THE ORANGERY OF THE CHÂTEAU

253   THE GRAND TRIANON

267   THE PETIT TRIANON

284   THE GARDENS OF THE PETIT TRIANON

302   THE QUEEN'S HAMLET

314   Bibliography

315   Quotation Sources

316   Index

319   Acknowledgments and Photographic Credits

"At first a closely guarded secret, his [Louis XIV's] love for Madame de La Vallière occasioned frequent excursions to Versailles, then a little castle of cards built by Louis XIII.... The King, his son ... built this little Versailles so he might enjoy greater intimacy with his mistress, pleasures unknown to the Just [Louis XIII]—that worthy son of St. Louis. By degrees, Louis XIV's tryst gave rise to the immense buildings here erected. Their convenience for his vast court, so different from the apartments at Saint-Germain, meant that shortly before the death of the queen, he would move there completely."

SAINT-SIMON, *Mémoires*, 1715.

FACING PAGE This bronze equestrian statue of Louis XIV dates from the nineteenth century. Erected in 1836 in the reign of Louis-Philippe on the site of the royal gateway that had been melted down during the Revolution, it has recently been restored and now stands enthroned on the *Place d'Armes* in front of the château entrance. The statue of the king is by Louis Petitot, while Pierre Cartellier is responsible for the horse. The latter was originally intended for an equestrian monument to Louis XV, which explains why, on closer inspection, the present incumbent appears rather too tall for his mount. It is fitting that, nearly three centuries after his death, the Sun King once again greets the six million visitors who flood into Versailles each year.

LOUIS XIV

1638 – 1715

FOREWORD

Catherine Pégard

President of the Public Establishment of the Château, Museum, and National Estate of Versailles

A private invitation to Versailles? The very idea might seem like a cute come-on. How could you possibly dwell, alone, on the lacy details of a sculpture, on the refinement of all those fabrics, on the hidden mechanisms of some piece of furniture? How could you venture onto the roof of the Royal Chapel, or slip behind the stage of the Opera House? How could you wander in the attic, or through the groves? How, in short, could you take the time to discover a château and grounds where you can never, ordinarily, be alone?

This handsome book extends such an invitation. But it is not just sheaves of glossy paper designed to show us the unseen. It truly stirs the emotions, creating a sense of *déjà-vu.* Whether you have often strolled through the Hall of Mirrors and along the edge of the Grand Canal, or are seeing the Queen's Bedchamber for the first time, an indescribable feeling will convince you that you're in familiar surroundings. Echoes of fading voices, reflections of lives past: the power of imagination. Everywhere, you'll see things—in your own way. Everything to be seen, all at once, overmuch. Yet only a few images will remain: some details from all those accumulated artworks, or an allusion to your own unique story buried in all those layers of history. A head of state may dwell on the monarch's majestic bearing, a Japanese woman might marvel at Marie-Antoinette's wardrobe, or an American be stirred by the battle of Yorktown.

And yet whoever we are, we're all struck by a shaft of sunlight in a shadowy room, by the shimmer of a chandelier, the gleam of bronze, or a sunset that paints the porphyry columns of the Grand Trianon. Every shade of light vaunts the special ambience of Versailles. The multiple beauties of Versailles beguile us, making us forget its universal attraction. Francis Hammond's subtle photographs bring time to a halt. His pictures spark memories, reviving emotions or spurring the desire to experience new ones. Guillaume Picon's carefully crafted text and quotations seem to have been expressly written for each image, bridging all gaps in time. I must therefore express my gratitude to Flammarion for having brought these two Versailles-loving "guides" together. And I must thank them for inviting us to share their passion in so wonderful a way.

FACING PAGE A trompe-l'œil medallion, one of the decorative elements on the ceiling in the Hall of Mirrors. The head of Apollo, the Sun, one of the symbols of Louis XIV, is surmounted by the *couronne fermée*—the crown of the kings of France—above which runs the royal motto *Nec pluribus impar*—understood to mean: "None is like unto him."
PAGES 12–13 Instantly recognizable with its marble paving and stone-and-brick architecture, the Marble Court is regarded as Louis XIII's principal legacy to Versailles.

INTRODUCTION

Laurent Salomé

Director of the National Museum of the Versailles and Trianon Palaces

*L*ooking through a window, over the back of a "rustic" chair (which is, in fact, an incredibly refined object with scrollwork and ears of wheat painted for the queen "in the colors of truth and nature," crowned by delightful little pine cones), and then catching a glimpse of the Temple of Love with its weeping willow, inevitably triggers one of those exquisite twinges of melancholy that can be experienced only at Versailles. A splendid book like this one makes it possible to relive, or imagine, the fleeting emotions that come one after another during a visit here. The constant brushes with perfection are astonishing, even as they create an intense desire to return to this timeless place. But being able to enjoy so many pleasures just by leafing through the pages of a book required long days of patrolling through the buildings and grounds of Versailles, taking care to be at just the right spot in just the right light, without overlooking the tiny detail that generates a sublime experience. Here Francis Hammond's inspired lens guarantees that nothing will be missed, while Guillaume Picon's brief yet evocative commentary gives the reader's imagination free rein.

The impression of suspended animation, of eternity, is paradoxical in a place that has always been full of frantic life and has never let a month go by without some spectacular change. Versailles is a perpetual construction site that crystallizes changes in tastes, customs, and concepts of authority. The best-informed readers will even recognize certain details that already belong to the past. The book's serene tone offers insight, in palimpsest, into the bustling saga of Versailles, into the tension between the personal and the historic. It also includes excursions into the nineteenth century—that other "grand century" at Versailles—which we trust will better reveal the palace's charms as the History Galleries founded by King Louis-Philippe recover their own special poetry and splendor.

Nothing can replace the pleasure of a beautiful book. This one is so carefully crafted that the magic works instantly: just turning its pages evokes scents of silk, cool marble, and waxed floors mingling with the fragrance of flowers outdoors, wafting on a gentle breeze.

FACING PAGE View of the Marble Hall leading out to the Marble Court.
PAGES 16–17 Looking on to the château, garden front.

The Château de VERSAILLES

If the Château de Versailles is first and foremost associated with Louis XIV,
the history of the palace starts with Louis XIII, who had a stone-and-brick residence built there in 1623.
This early palace was to be overhauled and enlarged a few years later, between 1631 and 1634.
Under Louis XIV, major building works started in 1661. The king moved the court wholesale
to the château in 1682 and the royal residence remained the seat of government until October 6, 1789,
the day the royal family was forced to return to Paris.

FACING PAGE Carved in 1680 by Martin Desjardins (born Van den Bogaert, in Breda, Holland),
Diana or *The Evening Hour* seems to have leapt off the fountain of
The Battle between the Animals and be striding toward the garden front of the château.
PAGE 20 Side corridor in the lower gallery, located on the ground
floor of the central range, beneath the Hall of Mirrors (the *Galerie des Glaces*).
PAGE 21 View through to the gardens from the Marble Hall across the lower gallery and corridor.

"I asked her if she would like to go with me to Versailles. She had the charming quality of being always ready for anything; perhaps because she had become accustomed in the past to spend half her time as the guest of other people.… In a minute she was ready before I had put on my greatcoat, and we went to Versailles."

☉

MARCEL PROUST, *In Search of Lost Time*.

FACING PAGE Enfilade leading out from the Council Chamber. The black-and-white tiling in Louis XVI's bathroom is visible, with, in the far distance, a door opening into the Geography Room, formerly the Gold Cabinet.

THE STAIRCASES
of Versailles

*The château boasts nearly seventy staircases. The grandest of them serve the main apartments,
while those of lesser importance connect various levels and rooms more discreetly.
The most opulent of them all, the Staircase of the Ambassadors, no longer exists, although the Queen's Staircase
remains and is similarly built in marble. In addition to these, more sober stairways illustrate stereotomy
à la française—that is, the art of cutting and assembling elaborate stonework.*

FACING PAGE The Staircase of Provence in the south wing served the apartments
of the Comte and Comtesse de Provence. The Comte de Provence, younger brother of Louis XVI,
ascended to the throne of France in 1814 as Louis XVIII.

TOP, LEFT The staircase, known in the nineteenth century as that of the "Dupes," dates to Louis XIV's reign.

TOP, RIGHT Louis XV ordained that the staircase called the *Petit Degré* be reserved for his sole personal use. In 1765, he had an "optical lantern" set up to light the lower part of the stairway.

BOTTOM, LEFT Semicircular, the staircase allows access from the ground floor up to the attic story.

BOTTOM, RIGHT One of the two spiral staircases in the Royal Chapel.

FACING PAGE Spiral staircase seen from the northern tribune (or gallery) of the second floor of the chapel.

FACING PAGE, ABOVE, AND PAGES 30-31 The marble staircase was one of the last embellishments to the apartment occupied
by Louis XIV's wife, Maria Theresa. Architect Jules Hardouin-Mansart oversaw the construction in 1680 after plans by François Le Vau
and by his de facto successor, François d'Orbay. Although known down the ages as the Queen's Staircase, it nonetheless serves
the King's Apartments. Its location soon made it the busiest stairway in Versailles, soon outdoing the Staircase of the Ambassadors.
The sumptuous decor is composed of marbles of various hues and from different quarries in the kingdom,
as decreed by the king and Colbert as part of their drive to see nationally sourced marble from the Pyrenees oust Italian imports.
ABOVE The landing on the first floor of the Queen's Staircase is adorned with a gilt-lead sculpture showing two amoretti carrying
an escutcheon bearing the interlaced ciphers of Louis XIV and his wife. Above the coat-of-arms, a pair of doves and the torches of Hymen,
the god of wedlock. The sculpture symbolizes the marriage between Louis XIV and Maria Theresa.

"The steps of the staircase are advancing well and I hope they will be entirely completed by July." "I will be well pleased when the great staircase is finished."

❧

Letter from **COLBERT** to the king, dated March 1, 1678, and **LOUIS XIV**'s reply from Ghent, where he was commanding a siege.

*T*he construction of this "grand staircase," on whose progress Louis XIV kept such a watchful eye, lasted for nearly ten years, from 1669 to 1678. It was an exceptional construction that mobilized many notable artists working on the great enterprise of Versailles—above all Charles Le Brun, *premier peintre du Roi* (first painter to the king). It bore the name Staircase of the Ambassadors, as delegates would mount it on their way to submit their letters of accreditation or to attend an audience with the king. The walls and framework were adorned with Rance and Languedoc marble trim over a white ground in the same stone; the treads were also in marble. The interior was complemented by a fountain and by a ceiling by Le Brun teeming with allegories to the glory of the sovereign that formed a prelude to the iconographical program of the Hall of Mirrors. In what was a technical tour de force for the time, the staircase was lit from above by a glazed canopy.

In this case, however, magnificence proved no guarantee of longevity. In 1750, Louis XV ordered the *grand escalier* of his great-grandfather to be dismantled. After its demolition in 1752, the stairway did, however, achieve a bizarre kind of posterity in the form of the late-nineteenth-century replica that Ludwig II of Bavaria—a monarch obsessed by Louis XIV and Versailles—set up in his castle of Herrenchiemsee.

FACING PAGE Mooted in 1772, the *Grand Degré* (or Gabriel Staircase) was only erected two centuries later, in 1985, after plans left by Ange-Jacques Gabriel, *premier architecte du Roi* (first architect to the king).

The King's SUITE

Created in the early 1670s, the grand appartement *or State Apartment of the king was composed of a luxurious suite of seven lavishly decorated halls, such as the Mercury and Apollo Rooms. Following the death of the queen, Louis XIV had a new apartment laid out at the back of the Marble Court that was used by the king and his successors until 1789. This was dubbed the* grand appartement *and became the venue for functions and royal entertainments. The throne room was installed in the Apollo Room.*

FACING PAGE The north end of the Hall of Mirrors. Late in the day, the failing light flits across a sumptuous marble-and-bronze decor, complete with statues, gueridons, and flambeaus fitted with girandoles that act as a counterpoint to the chandeliers hanging from the vaulted ceiling above.

ABOVE Completed in 1736 and opening in 1739 with a full-dress ball, the Hercules Room owes its name to the ceiling painted by François Lemoyne depicting the *Apotheosis of Hercules*. TOP AND BOTTOM, LEFT *The Feast at the House of Simon*, painted by Paolo Veronese in about 1570, was presented in 1664 to Louis XIV by the Republic of Venice, who were anxious to acquire support from the most powerful king in Christendom in their struggle against the Turkish infidel. BOTTOM, RIGHT Veronese's *Eleazar and Rebecca*, with an impressive frame by sculptor Jacques Verberckt, stands above the fireplace. FACING PAGE The dedication to Hercules is abundantly clear from the room's decor. Leaning on his famous bludgeon, the god appears in a medallion, while his head framed by the skin of the Nemean lion adorns the mantelpiece.

" The *grand appartement*, that is, from the gallery
to the platform, was decked out in crimson velvet
with golden tassels and fringes. One fine morning, they
were all found to have been cut off. This was nothing
short of miraculous in a place so busy in the day
and so shut up at night, and closely guarded at all times....
Five or six days afterwards, I was attending the king's
supper.... As dessert arrived, I saw—I wasn't sure
what I saw, something rather big and sort of black
in the air above the table.... The noise it made as it fell
and the weight of the thing could have made a dent, and
the plates leapt into the air, though none tumbled over,
and only by chance did the thing land on the tablecloth
and not in a dish. Hearing the impact, the king half
turned his head, and, without betraying the least emotion:
'I gather,' he said, 'that those are my fringes.'"

⚓

SAINT-SIMON, *Mémoires*, 1699.

FACING PAGE The *Salon de l'Abondance* (Hall of Plenty) led to Louis XIV's cabinet of curiosities,
which contained, among other things, his lavish collection of medals. They were stored in special cabinets
epitomized by this magnificent medal cabinet by André-Charles Boulle. Above it hangs a portrait
of the Duke of Burgundy (the king's eldest grandson) by Hyacinthe Rigaud.

"An 'Apartment,' as it was called, was an assemblage
of the entire court in the grand salon from seven
until ten o'clock in the evening, when the king
would sit down to table in the *grand appartement*,
in one of the withdrawing rooms at the end of the great
hall leading to the chapel. First would come music;
then tables were placed in all the rooms for
all kinds of gambling; there was lansquenet, at which
Monseigneur and Monsieur always played;
and also a billiard table; in a word, everyone
was free to play with whomever, and to ask for fresh
tables when the others were occupied.
Beyond the billiard room there was a refreshment hall,
and all was particularly well lit."

❧

SAINT-SIMON, *Mémoires*, 1692.

FACING PAGE The Peace Room as it appears from the Hall of Mirrors.

FACING PAGE Above, a large trophy emerges from the parti-colored marble lining (in white, green, and red) in the War Room, while below, the double "L" of the king's cipher appears framed by palm fronds and laurels.
ABOVE Framed by two pilasters, the bust of Emperor Domitian stands out against the marble ground and gilt-bronze decor. With a porphyry head and onyx robes, this bust came from the collection that Cardinal Mazarin bequeathed to his godson Louis XIV.

"In the evening [on the day of the wedding
of the dauphin, future Louis XVI, to Marie-Antoinette],
all assembled in the well-appointed gallery. Most remarkable
were the superb gilt busts bearing girandoles. The king
appeared at half past six and started playing at a very large
round table in the center. Everywhere the ladies gathered
in groups, which, together with the remaining courtiers
and some foreigners, filled the whole gallery with
the most superb attire. The balustrade was left open
for the ladies of Paris, who passed by one after the other
and put on a splendid show on the other side."

DUC DE CROŸ, *Journal inédit*, 1770.

PAGES 44-45 The Hall of Mirrors seen from the War Room.
FACING PAGE This view from the War Room provides a good idea of the sheer size of the seventy-three-meter-long Hall of Mirrors.
Construction started in 1678 but it was only completed six years later, the decoration of the vault occupying
Charles Le Brun and his workshop for nearly four years, from 1681 to 1684. The first painter to the king created an extraordinary
performance, a veritable epic to the glory of Louis XIV's historic deeds. The primary function of a gallery is to link other spaces,
but the sumptuously adorned Hall of Mirrors soon became the preferred venue for court entertainments and festivals in its own right.
PAGE 48 A chandelier in the Hall of Mirrors. PAGE 49 Behind a girandole on a stand, a statue of Venus dating
from antiquity forms a fine contrast with the marble cladding.

The Queen's SUITE

*After the death of Queen Maria Theresa in 1683, her apartment was taken over
by two dauphines, Maria Anna of Bavaria, and then by Marie Adelaide of Savoy. In the eighteenth century,
this* grand appartement *was again occupied by two queens, Marie Leszczinska, wife of Louis XV,
and by Marie-Antoinette. In certain rooms major alterations were made to the decor; for Marie-Antoinette,
for instance, the Queen's Bedchamber was totally refurnished and a new fireplace installed.*

PAGES 50-51 Under Louis XIV, the Venus Room marked the entrance to the King's Apartment.
The double door opened onto the imposing Staircase of the Ambassadors (see p. 32).
FACING PAGE The bust of Marie-Antoinette by Félix Lecomte.

FACING PAGE Marie-Antoinette took delivery of this splendid jewelry armoire from Ferdinand Schwerdfeger in 1787; the bronzes are by Thomire. The half-open door leads to the Bull's-Eye Room (the *Salon de l'Œil-de-Bœuf*), the second antechamber of the King's Apartment. Marie-Antoinette was to take this passageway on the morning of October 6, 1789, in making her escape from the revolutionary mob and hurrying to the king's side. Louis XVI had already gone on ahead of the queen, but he had taken the passage of the king, a suspended walkway that allowed the king to go to the queen without being observed. The couple thus missed each other by just minutes, adding further confusion to an already tumultuous situation. ABOVE A striking space, the Queen's Bedchamber is the most impressive room in the whole apartment. Her Majesty would actually sleep in this room—unlike the king, who, starting with Louis XV, only occupied his for the ceremonies of the royal *lever* (the "levee," when the king rose from bed) and *coucher* (when His Majesty returned to bed). Thus at night, the king could pay a visit to the queen in her bedchamber whenever he saw fit. Most important of all, it was in this room that the queen would be delivered of the royal offspring, "the children of France," her public confinement ensuring there could be no subterfuge or doubt surrounding the birth.

*S*uch as it is seen today, the Queen's Bedchamber is a composite, an attempt to restore it to its state on the morning of October 6, 1789, when Marie-Antoinette made her hurried departure. Some of the elements are original and attest to the presence of at least one of the three queens who occupied the room: Maria Theresa, Marie Leszczinska, or Marie-Antoinette. This is the case for the carved and painted ornaments on the ceiling and walls, the mantelpiece, the screen and fire-guard, the bedspread, and the jewelry dresser. The hanging in the alcove, as well as the embroidery on the bed and chairs, are authentic reconstructions. The textile was rewoven in 1946 and reinstated two years later. It is a piece for summer use, a fabric that is set up for only part of the year, from spring to fall. The fabric, delivered to Marie-Antoinette by Desfarges in 1787, presents a pattern with bouquets of flowers, ribbons, and peacock feathers. It too hung in the Queen's Bedchamber on October 6, 1789. Other reconstructions are based on archives but do not exclude a degree of improvisation; the crown-skirt over the bed, for example, and the edging round the wall hanging.

FACING PAGE Tester surmounted by ostrich plumes over the bed in the Queen's Bedchamber.

"Madame, daughter of King [Louis XVI],
came into the world before noon on December 19 [1778].
Etiquette, which demanded that all without distinction
presenting themselves at the time of the queen's
giving birth are permitted entrance, was so scrupulously
observed that the second the obstetrician Vermont
cried out: 'The queen is in labor,' the inquisitive crowd
that hurried to the bedchamber was so large and so unruly that
it was thought the crush might do the queen mischief."

𝒬

MADAME CAMPAN, *Mémoires de Madame Campan,* first lady of the chamber to Marie-Antoinette.

FACING PAGE Detail of the screen in the Queen's Bedchamber; it was delivered
in 1787 by Hauré and returned to Versailles only in 1939.

The Royal
CHAPEL

*The Royal Chapel was consecrated at the end of the reign of Louis XIV on June 5, 1710
by the archbishop of Paris. It was the fifth chapel the Sun King would have attended, though it was
the only one built at Versailles. Sovereign by divine right, the king of France, and with him the entire court,
attended Mass every day. The king and his family took their place in the royal tribune (or gallery),
while the public made do with the nave.*

FACING PAGE Side door opening into the chapel nave.
PAGES 62-63 Outside view of the Royal Chapel.

"[The chaplain] M. de Metz, as I have said, went
to see the new chapel with these gentlemen,
and Fornaro, to discover how he judged it, and the better
to view it with him. Soured by the Orléans affairs,
as well as struck by the quantity, magnificence, and opulence
of all the gold, paintings, and sculptures, he could not
prevent himself from averring that the king would do better,
and that it might stand better in the eyes of God,
to pay his starving troops rather than to pile up
so many glorious objects at the cost of the blood of his
wretched people perishing under the burden of taxes."

SAINT-SIMON, *Mémoires*, 1710.

FACING PAGE One of the doors leading from the royal gallery to an adjacent secondary gallery. At intervals during the divine office,
the king and his family would kneel on ceremonial hassocks dotted about the Savonnerie carpet. The bas-relief above
the door shows *Jesus at the Temple Instructing the Doctors of the Law*, a scene from the childhood of Christ by Guillaume Coustou.
PAGES 66-67 The decoration on the chapel ceiling is organized around three principal components, each representing
one of the three persons of the Trinity. In the center, Antoine Coypel painted *Our Eternal Father in his Glory Bringing
the Promise of Salvation to the World*, while, to the left in the half-dome of the apse, Charles de La Fosse illustrated
The Resurrection of Christ. On the opposite side above the royal gallery, Jean Jouvenet painted *The Descent of the Holy Spirit
upon the Virgin and the Apostles*. The ceilings in the side bays around the perimeter feature the twelve apostles.

*E*mbarked upon in 1689, the works for the new Royal Chapel were completed only twenty years later, in 1710. Between these two dates, the wars waged in the king's name starved such conspicuously costly items of funds. The inevitable delay, however, ill served the plans. Had it been finished ten or fifteen years earlier, the chapel would surely have been entirely dressed in marble and would have borne all the hallmarks of the Grand Siècle. The beginning of the new century gave rise instead to a resolutely modern building. The choice of materials (stone from the Île-de-France region replacing marble), the decor—interior and external, carved as well as painted—all testify to the fact. The structure of the Royal Chapel performs a delicate balancing act between glass and stone. It is tempting too to see the incipient influence here of Gothic art, in particular that of the Sainte-Chapelle built by St. Louis in the thirteenth century—especially since Louis XIV dedicated this new place of worship to the "Saint Roi," custodian and forefather of the Bourbon dynasty.

FACING PAGE An eighteenth-century copy of Titian's *The Pilgrims at Emmaus* hangs in the wood-paneled sacristy.

PAGE 70, FACING PAGE, AND ABOVE The organ mechanism is the work of Robert Clicquot, while the case was carved and gilded by five master craftsmen of the period: Taupin, Degoullons, Bellan, Lalande, and Le Goupil. From late 1763 to the beginning of 1764, a young Wolfgang Amadeus Mozart traveled to France and was received at court. On January 1, 1764, the composer and his family were invited to join the king's table. At the end of the meal, Louis XV asked to hear the young wunderkind. The impatient monarch left the table and strode off to the royal chapel with the little group hurrying after him. Mozart took his seat at the organ and started to play, unleashing a torrent of harmony from the pipes of the great instrument that, it is said, left the king dumbfounded.

PAGE 71 Wooden benches standing either side of the organ.

"The king [Louis XV], preceded by the princes
and M. le Dauphin, who offered his arm to the dauphine,
made their way to the chapel in a great procession, followed by
seventy lords and ladies of the court. The entrance to the chapel
and the whole august ceremony made a more glorious
sight than I would have believed possible. The couple were
on kneelers at the foot of the altar, with the king at
his prie-dieu and set well back; thirty-five ladies
of the court and the attendants made for a superbly attired
cortege to both sides…. Officiating was the Archbishop
of Reims, who performed the wedding ceremony. The king
and the entire royal family with the princes and princesses
formed groups behind. The newlyweds looked
not at all awkward, and everything went off with good grace."

☙

DUC DE CROŸ, *Journal inédit*, May 16, 1770.

FACING PAGE Looking down the chapel nave from the royal platform.

FACING PAGE View of the southern tribune (or gallery) of the Royal Chapel.
ABOVE One of the panels of the door leading to the royal gallery, featuring the king's monogram,
an entwined double "L" beneath a fleur-de-lis crown.

The King's APARTMENT

When Louis XIV transferred the court to Versailles in 1682, the queen and king disposed of one suite and petit appartement *each. Communicating with its grander counterpart, the "small apartment" allowed the sovereigns to escape for a time from the demands of the protocol that governed every ritual of court life. Following the death of the queen, Louis XIV forsook the State Apartments. Turned into a reception room for a new suite of rooms, they became the focus of the king's public life and the theater of the ceremonies of the* lever *and the* coucher.

FACING PAGE From the Hall of Mirrors, a view through to the king's second anteroom, called the Bull's-Eye Room.

"Speaking here of etiquette, I do not just mean the order incumbent on majesty that governs every court on ceremonial occasions. I'm speaking about the minute rules that pursue our kings in their most private affairs, in their hours of suffering as in those of pleasure, right down to their most repugnant human infirmities."

MADAME CAMPAN, *Mémoires de Madame Campan,* first lady of the chamber to Marie-Antoinette.

FACING PAGE In the evening, leaving the apartment of Madame de Maintenon as the clock struck ten, Louis XIV, accompanied by *Les Symphonies pour les Soupers du Roi* composed by Delalande (superintendent of the royal chamber music), would take his supper in public in the first *Grand Couvert*, anteroom. The paintings decorating this antechamber were carried out by Joseph Parrocel between 1685 and 1688 and show battles from antiquity. The picture visible here represents a cavalry charge taking place before the ramparts of a besieged city.

ABOVE AND FACING PAGE The king's second anteroom, the Bull's-Eye Room (the *Salon de l'Œil-de-Bœuf*)
derives its name from the oval bull's-eye window (*œil-de-bœuf*) that opens in the curved ceiling. It was in this
antechamber that courtiers would wait to be conducted into the king's chamber.

In 1701, Louis XIV had his bedchamber installed in the King's Room, which had once served to separate the King's Apartment from that of the queen, and which had been overhauled in 1678 during works on the Hall. The King's Bedchamber thus now stood at the center of the château.

The key moments in the royal "liturgy" were celebrated here, including the daily ceremonies of the king's *lever* and the *coucher*. At half past eight, the *premier valet de chambre* (or first valet-in-waiting) approached the king's bed and announced: "Sire, the hour has come!" The king's day would start with a private *petit lever*, followed by the public *grand lever* half an hour later. Between ten and eleven in the morning, the king would go to the Royal Chapel to attend Mass. The king's daily routine thus ran like clockwork, concluding only some time between eleven and midnight, when the king regained his bedchamber for the ceremony of the *coucher*. These rituals only fell into disuse with the departure of Louis XVI and Marie-Antoinette for the Tuileries in 1789.

Louis XIV died in Versailles on September 1, 1715, having received extreme unction on August 25, the feast day of St. Louis, patron of the dynasty.

FACING PAGE The King's Bedchamber possesses a uniquely characteristic decor.
The giltwood balustrade dates from Louis-Philippe's reign. It separates the alcove where the king's bed stood from the rest of the room. On the delicately coffered tympanum above the baldachin is a low-relief carved by Nicolas Coustou entitled *France Watching over the King's Sleep*.

"At eight, the *premier valet de chambre* [first valet-in-waiting] on duty, who had slept alone in the king's [Louis XIV] bedchamber and who was already dressed, would wake him. The court physician, court surgeon, and, for as long as she was alive, his wetnurse would enter at the same time. She would go and kiss him; the others would rub him down, and often change his shirt, as he was prone to sweating. On the quarter-hour, the Grand Chamberlain was called, or, in his absence, the first gentleman of the bedchamber for the year, and, with them, the *grandes entrées* [the most distinguished personalities of the court]."

SAINT-SIMON, *Mémoires*, 1715.

FACING PAGE Detail of the furnishing fabric that lined the walls of the alcove and the canopy bed in the King's Bedchamber. This fabric was made in Lyon in the second half of the twentieth century, based on a magnificent gold and silver brocade cloth on crimson ground delivered to the court between 1731 and 1733 by Bron and Ringuet. The reconstruction operation took nearly twenty-five years and required the skills of two Lyon firms, Prelle and Tassinari & Chatel.

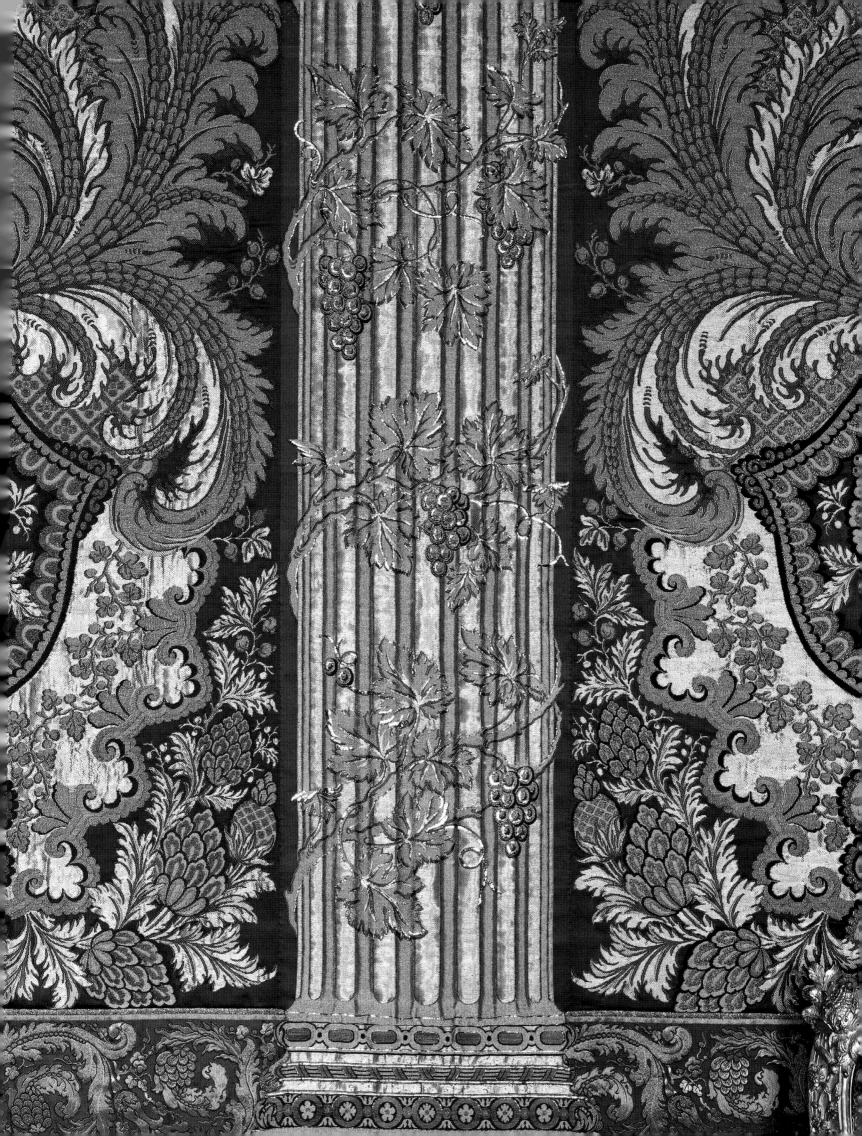

"On Wednesday August 28 [1715], he [Louis XIV] proffered an amiable remark to Madame de Maintenon which she cannot be said to have relished and to which she replied not a word. He had only told her that he took comfort from the hope that, given his age, they would meet again soon enough. At seven o'clock in the morning, he had Father Tellier called in and, as the latter spoke to him of God, he saw in the mirror above his mantelpiece two boys of the bedchamber squatting at the foot of the bed, weeping. He said to them: 'Why are you crying? Did you think I was immortal? I never believed so myself, and you, seeing the age I've reached, should have steeled yourselves to losing me.'"

SAINT-SIMON, *Mémoires*, 1715.

FACING PAGE On one of the fireplaces in the King's Bedchamber is a bust of Louis XIV by Antoine Coysevox. The bust is flanked by two candelabras that once belonged to Louis XVI's brother, the Comte de Provence, who later became Louis XVIII.

The King's
PRIVATE APARTMENT

*Initially, Louis XIV had his Private Apartment (*appartement intérieur*) laid out as a suite of rooms to display the royal collection of paintings. In 1735, Louis XV decided to transform the gallery into a residential apartment where, free for a moment from the demands of etiquette, he might enjoy peace and quiet. The greatest artists and craftsmen of the age were summoned to design and execute its decor. It was here that both Louis XV and Louis XVI preferred to work with their ministers and trusted advisers.*

FACING PAGE In 1738, Louis XV had a new bedchamber set up in what had been Louis XIV's billiard room. Above the lintel hangs a painting of Louise Élisabeth of France, Infante of Spain and then Duchess of Parma, by the workshop of Jean-Marc Nattier. Louis XV died here on May 10, 1774, while Louis XVI occupied the room until his forced departure from Versailles on October 6, 1789.

TOP, RIGHT AND BOTTOM, LEFT The finely carved wooden trim in the dressing room by the Rousseau brothers was made for Louis XVI in 1788. Presented here are the attributes of the Navy and the Arts. TOP, LEFT AND BOTTOM, RIGHT Two bas-reliefs in bronze of *Love the Actor* and *Confidence* adorning the thuja burl casements on a dresser from the dressing room.

ABOVE Standing in front of wood paneling carved by the Rousseau brothers,
an armchair from a set produced by the Foliots in about 1770. Completed for Queen Marie-Antoinette
at the Château de Choisy, it was partially moved to Louis XVI's dressing room in 1788.

ABOVE The Stags Court seen from a window in the King's dressing room.
FACING PAGE Far from the ceremonial formality of the State Apartments, Louis XV would invite to supper those who had accompanied him out hunting to the "Return from the Hunt" dining room. Admission was strictly regulated and regarded as a special honor. A bust of Louis XVI stands on a chest of drawers by Étienne Levasseur that has since been transferred to the Louvre.
PAGE 96 A detail of the woodwork on the Clock Room, named for the astronomical timepiece displayed there.
PAGE 97 Louis XV had this tour de force of horology, made by the engineer Passemant, placed here in 1754. The mechanism had taken the clockmaker Dauthiau a dozen years to perfect and its bronze case was engraved by Caffieri after designs chosen by the king himself. More than just a clock, it is a veritable monument to the arts and the sciences and indicates, among other data, the hour, the day of the week, the month, and the year.

ABOVE AND FACING PAGE Louis XV was interested in science, in astronomy in particular, which explains
the presence of a copper rod marking the Paris meridian on the floor in the Clock Room.

The *cabinet intérieur* of Louis XV—also known as the *cabinet d'angle* or Corner Room—occupies part of Louis XIV's paintings gallery. The first alterations made by Louis XV to this bright, pleasantly located room date to 1735, with the installation of a fireplace in *griotte* marble, now surmounted by a rocaille-style overmantel carved by Verberckt and his workshop. In 1741, court observer Duc de Luynes noted in his *Mémoires* that the king was "almost always" to be found in his *cabinet intérieur*. Clearly the monarch enjoyed spending time there surrounded by gorgeous furniture. In 1739 Gaudreaux delivered a splendid *médaillier* (medal cabinet) that was joined in 1755 by two matching corner cabinets built by Joubert.

His study was quickly recognized as one of the most lavish rooms in the whole château, but in 1753 the king had changes made to its decor, with the crimson damask covering the walls being replaced by wood. Ten large panels were commissioned, among the finest in the Louis XV style in Versailles. In 1769, the furniture was further enriched by the famous "King's Desk." Under Louis XVI, the room remained a place of work and it was hung with portraits of the king and his forebears, as well as of Queen Marie-Antoinette. The bronze and porcelain "American Independence" candelabrum on the medal cabinet recalls one of the great events of the reign: the war waged against Great Britain in support of the rebellion.

Nonetheless, this room, envisaged by Louis XV as a place to which he could retreat, was soon invaded by courtiers, to the point that the king felt the need to make space for a more private study, or *arrière-cabinet*.

FACING PAGE View of the King's Study (*cabinet intérieur*).

*L*ouis XV required a bureau in which he could hide his private papers without having to put them in a drawer that would then have to be kept shut. The cylinder *secrétaire*, begun by the cabinetmaker Œben in 1760 and completed by his successor Riesener nine years later was the perfect response to this royal desire. Delivered by Riesener to the king in 1769, the desk, in which ormolu vies with exquisite marquetry, was said to have cost 62,000 *livres*, making it one of the most expensive pieces of furniture ever acquired by the Crown. It is certainly quite an exceptional piece and well deserving of the impressively regal name by which it is known: the *Bureau du Roi*. Exemplary in execution, the King's Desk also boasts a secret mechanism: to open the roll-top (composed of slats forming a quarter cylinder) and gain access to all the drawers, one has but to give the key a quarter-turn—hence why neither cylinder nor drawers are equipped with handles, since this ingenious contraption renders them superfluous. The vicissitudes of time and cruel fate however have not spared the King's Desk. Restored in a slapdash manner in the nineteenth century, to open the roll-top today one has to turn the key like crank-handle about a dozen times.

FACING PAGE Detail of Louis XV's roll-top desk in the King's Study.

102

ABOVE General view of the King's Desk with the roll-top raised. The wrought-iron key with which the desk can be opened
is decorated with two interlocking "L's and enclosed is a miniature enamel portrait of Louis XV, destroyed in the course of the Revolution.
FACING PAGE In the center of the desk a foldaway board hinged on a copper compass rod (left) conceals a space with three
secret drawers at the rear in which the king could store his personal papers with complete peace of mind.

ABOVE AND FACING PAGE The medal cabinet in the King's Study,
designed by Antoine Gaudreaux in 1738.

In 1780, a medal cabinet and two encoignures from Versailles were placed on deposit in the Royal Library. They were subsequently transferred with the furniture in the cabinet to the Medals Department at the Bibliothèque Nationale de France, and it was only in 1960 that this exceptional ensemble was restored to its erstwhile home in the King's Study within his Private Apartment. "A piece of furniture of extravagant luxury," the medal cabinet was built to store the "metal history" of Louis XV in the form of a numismatic collection celebrating the great events of the reign. The medal cabinet was carried out in 1738 by the cabinetmaker Antoine Gaudreaux after designs by the Slodtz brothers. In all probability such a design would have been approved by Louis XV himself. Characterized by supple forms and opulent bronzework, the piece is adorned with medals, a female mascaron, and entwined palm fronds, and clearly reflects the king's taste in the decorative arts. Two vases from the Royal Manufacture at Sèvres made for Louis XVI, and the "American Independence" candelabrum stand on the medal cabinet. Pendants to the cabinet, the corner cabinets were supplied by Gilles Joubert in 1755, their purpose being to store the overflow from the Gaudreaux chest. Less preciously crafted than the medal cabinet proper, the oval medallions are decorated in gilt bronze with children playing, and constitute a fine counterpoint to the wooden ornaments on the cabinet. On the example shown here, the putti illustrate Poetry; on the other the personification is of Music.

PAGES 108–9, AND FACING PAGE
The corner cabinets made by Gilles Joubert in 1755.

"Having been out hunting as was his wont,
the king marked me on his list that the usher read at the door.
Entry was selective, and one had to climb a back staircase
to get to the small cabinets…. After ascending,
one waited for supper to start in the small salon. The king came
only to sit at the table with the ladies. The dining room was
charming and the supper extremely agreeable and informal.
One was served by just two or three valets of the Wardrobe,
who withdrew after presenting whatever was to be placed
before one. Easefulness and decency appeared to me both
to be observed: the king was merry and relaxed, but always
with a grandeur that ensured it was never forgotten."

DUC DE CROŸ, *Journal inédit*, Paris, January 30, 1747.

FACING PAGE
View over the Marble Court through a window in the King's Study.

113

The Gold Plate Room does not derive its name from the piece of furniture, "surprising in its strangeness," which Louis XVI had set up there. His grandfather Louis XV liked to take coffee in this room. In fact coffee drinking was an activity that in no way detracted from the exercise of the kingly office. It was in what was once a private room used by Madame Adélaïde, Louis XV's daughter, that the king chose to display his collection of gold plate. It was embellished with new wood paneling between 1753 and 1767 by the sculptor Jacques Verberckt. Madame Adélaïde had turned it into a music-room in which she took Italian lessons with Goldoni and learned the harp from Beaumarchais.

It was there that Mozart was received by the king and Madame de Pompadour in December 1763 and gave a harpsichord recital. As the last chord faded, the young protégé manifested the desire to embrace the favorite. She flatly refused and the composer—who had after all been permitted to kiss Maria Theresa of Austria by the Empress herself—was left flabbergasted.

FACING PAGE Marble bust of the young Louis XV by Antoine Coysevox,
exhibited in the King's Suite.

ABOVE AND FACING PAGE Louis XVI's medal cabinet
standing in the Gold Plate Room, delivered to Louis XVI in c. 1788.

116

Delivered to Louis XVI in about 1788, this piece was listed as "*médaillier*" in the *Catalogue des meubles et effets précieux provenant de la ci-devant liste civile,* which was drawn up for the auction of the furniture from Versailles that ran from August 25, 1793 to August 11, 1794. "Dazzling in technique and regal in preciosity," this piece of furniture is absolutely unique, an objet d'art in its own right. A cabinet for medals or for some other usage, the wealth of precious details seems to belie its purpose as a storage unit. Take, for instance, the compositions on the medallions and the panels; set in wax, feathers and wings from butterflies or exotic birds are neatly arranged in the shape of birds, butterflies, and plants. This singularly original decor marks a clear break with the use of marble mosaic traditionally employed in this type of furniture. Acquired in 1796 by a supplier to the army for the sum of 3,000 *livres* (the 1793 inventory estimates it at 15,000), it went on sale in London in 1876 and entered the Rothschild collection. Thanks to legal provisions for gifts-in-lieu, in 1986 it rejoined the Versailles collection.

"In the reign of Louis XV, the King's Private Apartment was supplied with running water coming from the Montbauron reservoirs, the pressure being sufficient to reach the first floor of the château. It is almost certain that Louis XV's bathroom benefited from running tap water. The king disposed of two bathtubs. He would soap himself down in one and rinse himself in the other. The room with the tanks on the mezzanine possessed cisterns with hot and cold water."

FRÉDÉRIC DIDIER, Head Architect of the French Historic Monuments at the Château de Versailles, 2004.

FACING PAGE
Detail of the inlay in the *Cassette* (Purse Room).

ABOVE AND FACING PAGE Detail of the inlay in the *Cassette* (Purse Room)—at one time Louis XV's bathroom—where Louis XVI would keep his personal expenditure accounts. The carved decoration gilded in several tones (green, yellow, and red gold) illustrates the transitional idiom of the end of the reign of Louis XV heralding the new style that blossomed under his successor.

Marie-Antoinette's
PRIVATE ROOMS

Contrasting with her formal suite, from the seventeenth century the queen also made use of smaller, more private cabinets. At the time of Louis XIV, Queen Maria Theresa disposed solely of an oratory and a boudoir. Over time, however, the number of rooms increased. Louis XV's wife Marie Leszczinska liked to withdraw to her private rooms to read or take painting lessons from Jean-Baptiste Oudry. Marie-Antoinette had them entirely refurbished in keeping with the style of the day.

FACING PAGE
Detail of a bolt on one of the doors to the Sofa Room (*Cabinet de la Méridienne*).

124

"The moment he arrived in France, Gluck was permitted to attend on the Queen [Marie-Antoinette] as she dressed, and she proceeded to talk with him constantly throughout his stay. One day she asked him whether he was on the point of finishing his great opera *Armide* and whether he was satisfied with it. Gluck, with his German accent, answered her with great coolness: 'Madam, it will soon be finished and it really will be superb.' If candidly expressed, his opinion was later confirmed and the operatic art surely possesses not a single work of greater effect."

MADAME CAMPAN, *Mémoires de Madame Campan,*
first lady of the chamber to Marie-Antoinette.

FACING PAGE Marie-Antoinette also liked to retreat to the privacy of her *cabinet intérieur* and to the Gold Room
with her children and intimates. There she would take music lessons from Grétry, director
of the queen's music, or pose for the portraitist Madame Vigée-Lebrun, who in 1783, thanks to support from
her royal protector, was inducted into the Royal Academy of Painting and Sculpture. The current decor dates to 1783.
The paneling by the Rousseau brothers follows designs by Richard Mique, Marie-Antoinette's favorite architect.
The chairs by cabinetmaker Georges Jacob would have been provided specifically for this room.
From the wood carvings to the furniture, not forgetting the elegant bronze chandelier and the fire set beneath
the mantelpiece, the interior is entirely embellished in gold—whence the name *Cabinet Doré*—or Gold Room.

"She liked all that soothes, everything that is conducive
to daydreaming, all those joys that appeal to young
women and amuse youthful sovereigns alike: havens
of familiarity where friendship flows freely, intimate
conversations in which the mind lowers its guard, and Nature,
that friend, and the woods, those confidantes,
and the horizon, in which the eye and the spirit can plunge,
and flowers, with their eternal merriment."

☙

EDMOND AND JULES DE GONCOURT, *Histoire de Marie-Antoinette.*

FACING PAGE Detail of the harp exhibited in the Gold Room made by Jean Henri Nadermann,
master instrument maker to Marie-Antoinette.

The destiny of the Japanese lacquers owned by Marie-Antoinette is nothing short of astonishing and offers a striking contrast with that of the queen herself, guillotined on October 16, 1793. Happenstance or irony of history, these delicate objects emerged from the Revolution unscathed.

The royal couple left Versailles on October 6, 1789, never to return. A few days after her enforced departure, Marie-Antoinette asked the art dealer Daguerre to recover and return the lacquerwork then on display in the Gold Room. The majority was, at that time, given pride of place in a vitrine with nine shelves that Riesener had made to order for the queen. Some pieces, like the reclining puppy, stood on one of the tables either side of the fireplace. Daguerre's clerk Ligncreux hurried to Versailles and, on October 10, 1789, drew up an inventory of the collection running to sixty-eight items. The "lacquer cage" built by Riesener was removed on the occasion of the auction that disposed of the Versailles furniture (August 1793 to August 1794), and in 1794 the collection was transferred to the Muséum Central des Arts—the future Museum of the Louvre. It is composed of lacquerwork presented to or bought by the queen, together with that inherited from her mother, Maria Theresa, whose collection fell to Marie-Antoinette by bequest on the death of the Empress in 1780.

FACING PAGE This square, three-tier box borne on curved bracket feet comes from Marie-Antoinette's collection of Japanese lacquer. A large section cut out of the side reveals a geometric motif on each level.
ABOVE A late eighteenth-century inventory describes the other piece in the queen's lacquer collection shown here as a cat. It is in fact a box in the shape of a puppy lying on a miniature coffee table and was bought in 1777 at the sale of the receiver-general of finances (that is, inspector-general for tax), Randon de Boisset, a wealthy collector, later being sold on to the queen.

ABOVE Books from the library of the queen. The initials "CT" indicate that the books
once belonged to the queen's library in the Château de Trianon.
FACING PAGE The decoration on this Sèvres vase, exhibited in Marie-Antoinette's Gold Room, was painted
by Jean François Lécot, a major figure in the revival of the "Chinese" style in the 1770s.

ABOVE AND FACING PAGE In the former Poets' Room of Queen Marie Leszczinska, Marie-Antoinette
et up paneling painted in natural colors and enriched with *vernis Martin*. Decorated
with pastoral scenes, the wainscoting had been recovered from one of the private rooms belonging
to the late dauphine, Maria Josepha of Saxony, Louis XVI's mother.

134

"I do not want to have to wait for Compiègne before providing you with an account of my reading. I have for some time been engrossed in … [Pierre] L'Estoile's *Mémoires*. It is a journal of the reigns of Charles IX, Henry III, and Henry IV [of France]. One can see everything that took place at that time, day after day, the good and the ill deeds, the laws and the customs. I find there, the names, the offices, and sometimes the origins of people now at court. I'm still reading the *Lettres d'une mère à sa fille et de la fille à sa mère*; though diverting, they expound good principles and excellent morals."

☾

Letter from **MARIE-ANTOINETTE** to her mother, Empress Maria Theresa, July 17, 1772.

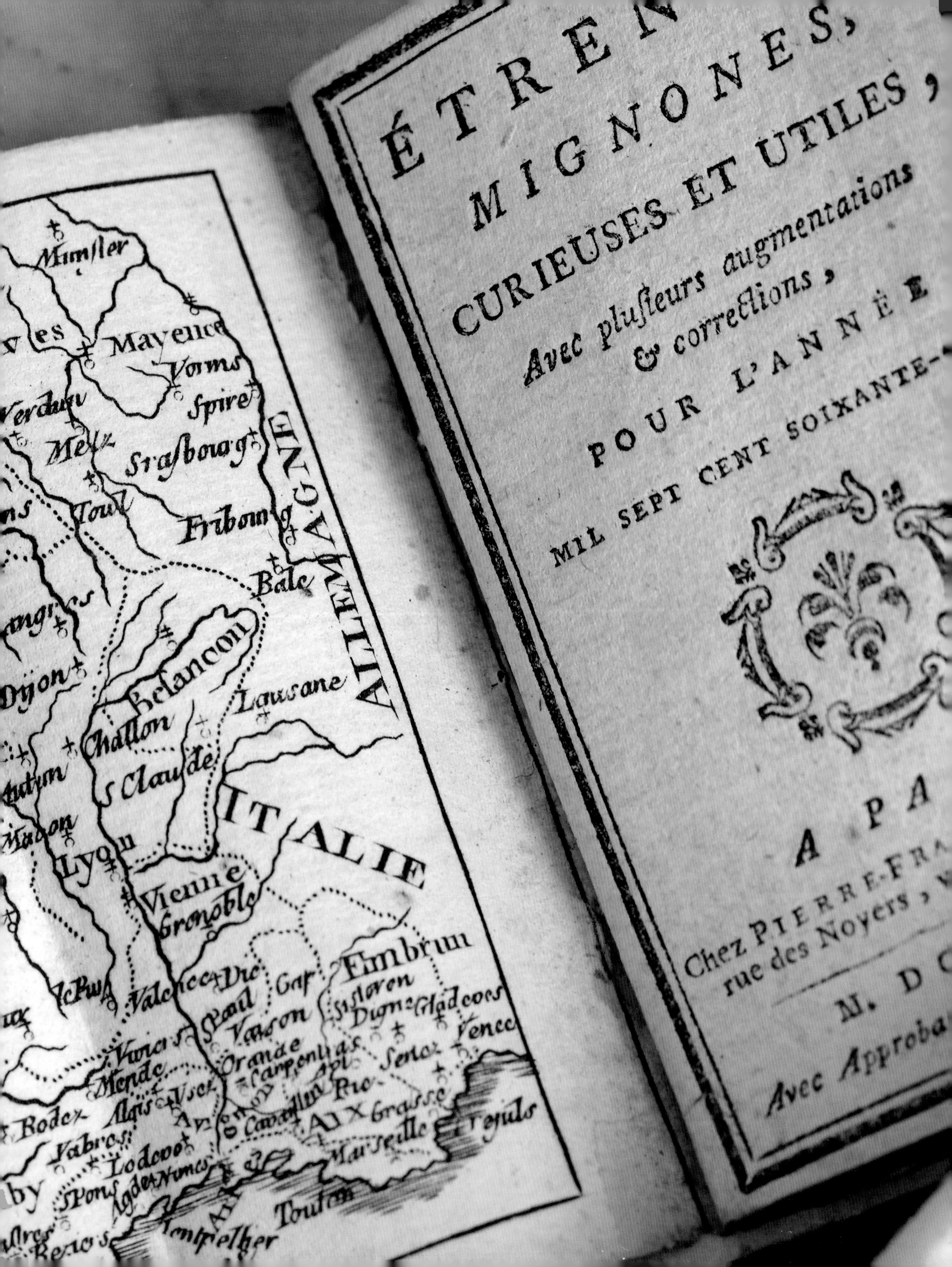
ÉTREN
MIGNONES,
CURIEUSES ET UTILES,
Avec plusieurs augmentations
& corrections,
POUR L'ANNÉE
MIL SEPT CENT SOIXANTE-
A PA
Chez PIERRE-FRA
rue des Noyers, v
M. DC
Avec Approba
Munster
Mayence
Vorms
Spire
Verdun
Strasbourg
Toul
Fribourg
Bale
ALLEMAGNE
Besançon
Dijon
Lausane
Challon
S Claude
Macon
ITALIE
Lyon
Vienne
Grenoble
Embrun
Valence
Gap
Sisteron
Vaison
Orange
Carpentras
Vence
Senez
Mende
Uzes
Alais
Rodez
Vabres
Lodeve
Cavaillon
AIX
Grasse
Frejus
Marseille
S Pons
Agde
Nimes
Toulon

FACING PAGE AND ABOVE The copy of *Étrennes mignonnes, curieuses et utiles ...*
pour l'année 1771—a kind of almanac, or compendium of information, advice, anecdotes,
and jokes for the year—once belonged to Marie-Antoinette when she was dauphine.

ABOVE A collection of hand-illustrated music manuscripts for harp, guitar, and piano. This one is dedicated to Her Royal Highness Princess of Piedmont—Madame (Marie) Clotilde of France, sister of Louis XVI and wife of Charles Emmanuel of Savoy.

FACING PAGE View of part of the Queen's Library. The room was furbished in 1772 for the dauphine, before being altered seven years later for the queen. One of the panels in the library is false, the fake binding concealing a secret door, here shown ajar.

"The Comtesse d'Artois was delivered on the 6th at a quarter to four in the most uncomplicated manner imaginable: she had only three serious birth pangs and, in all, the labor lasted barely two hours. I was in her chamber throughout: it is superfluous to tell my dear mama how much I suffered to see an heir who is not mine. I did, however, my utmost to administer with solicitude to mother and child. Will my dear mama see fit to accept the respect and tenderness of a daughter who is so distraught at having displeased her?"

Letter from **MARIE-ANTOINETTE** to her mother, Empress Maria Theresa, August 12, 1775.

The Sofa Room is an octagonal room with recessed doors in the sides that allowed the queen's chambermaids to leave her bedchamber to work in other rooms without disturbing the sovereign. The queen would often rest here, in general in the middle of the day—whence the name "meridian" given to the boudoir. In 1781, after Marie-Antoinette had finally given birth to a dauphin, the room was redecorated with new wood paneling.

FACING PAGE Designed by the Rousseau brothers, the woodwork in the Sofa Room
(*Cabinet de la Méridienne*) is full of meaning. The rose shoots running along the molding and the peacock
(an attribute of the goddess Juno) symbolize the marital love between the king and queen.

FACING PAGE On the console, a terracotta bust of Louis Charles, Duke of Normandy,
son of the royal couple and second dauphin after the death of his elder brother. The console table was made
in 1781 for this very room to celebrate the birth of Dauphin Louis, who died in June 1789.
ABOVE Details of furniture. TOP, LEFT A detail of the console presented in 1781. The medallion represents a dolphin (*dauphin*)
in a glory surrounded by flaming hearts, an allusion to the joyous birth on October 22, 1781 of the son that the king
and the queen had longed for. BOTTOM, LEFT A detail of an armchair supplied by Jacob in about 1785.
The armrest is decorated with a dog's head motif, an imaginative touch in a piece of this type.

FACING PAGE AND ABOVE While dauphine, in 1770, Marie-Antoinette had been presented with this Vienna-made
gueridon with a petrified wood top as a gift from her sister, Archduchess Maria Christina.
Acquired during the Revolution by a certain citizen Grincourt for 820 *livres*, after many vicissitudes,
in 1966 it rejoined Versailles by means of a bequest by Count Niel.

The Queen's
PRIVATE APARTMENT

Marie-Antoinette occupied a petit appartement *on the ground floor of the château comprising
three main rooms: bedchamber, bathroom, and library. Demolished under Louis-Philippe,
the suite was rebuilt in the twentieth century, except for the library. Her* grand appartement *being located
on the floor above, to enter the Private Apartment the queen would proceed along the King's Passage
and then take a stairway leading to what today constitutes the Marble Hall.*

FACING PAGE The Queen's Bedchamber in her Private Apartment.
On the wall is a picture by Louis Auguste Brun representing Marie-Antoinette on horseback,
riding not sidesaddle, but astride her mount like a man.

"As for our Court, it was completely under the thumb of the queen. It was M. Necker who had dismissed M. de Sartine, who, however, had set up the Navy and had M. de Castries named in his place; but it was the queen who got the better of M. de Maurepas, who was on the point of signing on M. de Puységur, and she had M. de Ségur nominated on December 23, 1780. Then there could be no doubt that she exerted her influence chiefly over the choice of ministers and the major appointments. Thus, everything ran through her and her circle, which at that time included Madame the Duchesse de Polignac, etc. The group was kindly and benevolent, and people spoke well of it. The king also appeared increasingly in love. It was then said that the queen was with child, so her position reached its apogee, and that of her coterie likewise."

DUC DE CROŸ, *Journal inédit*, 1780–1782.

FACING PAGE Terracotta bust of Louis Antoine d'Artois, Duke of Angoulême (1775–1844), as a child. Louis Antoine was the son of the Comte d'Artois, Louis XVI's second brother and future Charles X (r. 1824–1830). Louis Antoine grew up to become dauphin in his turn in 1824. In the mirror is reflected a picture by Madame Vigée-Lebrun depicting the queen's two elder children in 1784.
PAGE 152 Detail of the embroidered satin counterpane on Louis XVI's bed in the bathroom of the Queen's Private Apartment. The panels of the quilt are emblazoned with the interlaced initials of the king and queen.
PAGE 153 The bed was delivered in 1785 for the bathroom of Louis XVI at Compiègne, before being moved the following year to the king's bathroom at Fontainebleau. This piece of furniture is all the more interesting for its rarity value, since very few royal beds from before 1789 remain. Made by Boulard, it is a *lit à la polonaise* with head- and footboard and valance.
Starting from the mid-eighteenth century, personal hygiene made considerable advances. Hitherto bathing had been believed to dilate the pores of the skin and allow noxious substances to enter the body, gradually it lost this dubious reputation. Slowly but surely the practice of regular washing gained ground. In princely apartments, restrooms for use after the bath were installed. Louis XVI's bed thus provides material evidence of improvements in bodily hygiene at the end of the eighteenth century.

TOP, LEFT AND BOTTOM, RIGHT Details of the paneling in the bathroom of
the Queen's Private Apartment: a crayfish and a basin with two swans drinking.
TOP, RIGHT AND BOTTOM, LEFT Details of Louis XVI's bed.
The valance and the shell decor on one of the stiles carved by Hauré.

ABOVE Detail of the wood carving in the bathroom.
A veritable celebration of water and bathing, the decor of swan, reeds,
shells, and pearls suits the room's function to perfection.

THE APARTMENTS
of the Royal Mistresses

After the death of Madame de Châteauroux in 1744, her successor in Louis XV's heart, Madame de Pompadour, occupied an apartment located above the King's Suite. In 1751 the king's favorite moved to the ground floor. Madame Du Barry, Louis XV's last official mistress (from 1769 to the death of the king in 1774) lived in what were formerly the rooms of the king on the second floor, occupied by the dauphine from 1765 to 1767.

FACING PAGE This corner room was used for gaming by Louis XV's mistress Madame Du Barry.
PAGE 158 Detail in Madame Du Barry's library, laid out in 1756 initially for Louis XV's daughter, Madame Adélaïde.
PAGE 159 The enfilade leading from the bedroom to the corner room through
the *grand cabinet* of Madame Du Barry.

"Soon she [Mme Du Barry] was recognized
as the king's mistress and took over the apartment
of Madame de Pompadour, located above that of the king
and hitherto occupied by the Duc de Villequier.
It communicated with the king's via the staircase that
descended to the right of the Marble Court; but the real
entrance was by way of a narrow and ill-lit stairway;
and, though this apartment was far larger than many
in Versailles, it was rather inconvenient for in murky
weather several of its rooms had to be lit."

COMTE D'HÉZECQUES, *Souvenirs d'un page de la cour de Louis XVI*, 1873.

FACING PAGE Chair in gilded walnut delivered in 1769 for a room intended for Comtesse Du Barry's lady-in-waiting.
The wooden parts of this armless chair with its oval medallion back were made by Delanois. The upholstery
is not original but an attempt to reconstitute a chair covered in three different fabrics, of the kind the supplier
would present to the favorite, who could then choose her preferred fabric for all the other chairs. This was
by no means the reality, since the choice of fabric was taken beforehand from samples presented to whoever placed
the order. Once the selection had been made, the upholsterer, if ever it was deemed necessary to check
the ratio between textile and wood, would mount the fabric on the article. No evidence has been found that swatches
of various cloths would be sewn on to one and the same chair, since such a practice would have obscured
the relationship between the material and the wood.

ABOVE Plaster bust of Madame Du Barry dating from the nineteenth century, original by Pajou.
FACING PAGE The copper cage adorned with porcelain flowers once
occupied by Madame Du Barry's parrot.

ABOVE The marble fireplace surround in Madame de Pompadour's second anteroom. The mirror reflects
a 1746 portrait of the Marquise de Pompadour as Diana the huntress by Jean-Marc Nattier.
FACING PAGE Reconstruction of the bedchamber decorated in 1748 for Madame de Pompadour with Louis XV furniture
acquired by Versailles through various donations. The *à la Bourgogne* transformation table visible in the foreground
comes from the Duchess of Windsor bequest. The bed sits in an alcove. The wood paneling is by Verberckt.

THE APARTMENTS
of the Dauphin and Dauphine

As soon as Louis XIV moved into Versailles, the apartments named after the dauphin and dauphine were always reserved as a priority for the heir to the throne, the dauphin. Initially this was the elder son of Louis XIV, also called Monseigneur, and then that of Louis XV. Thereafter, Louis XVI allotted them to his brother and his wife, the Comte and Comtesse de Provence.
In 1787, the latter gave them up in favor of the dauphin, and then, on his death in 1789, his younger brother, the new dauphin and future Louis XVII, occupied them.

FACING PAGE The bedchamber of Louis (1729–1765), the dauphin, son of Louis XV, is adorned with a portrait
of his first wife, Maria Teresa Rafaela, Infanta of Spain (1726–1746), painted by Louis Michel Van Loo. The premature
death of this young princess, just a year after her marriage, profoundly saddened the dauphin.

"Madame the Dauphine, née Saxe, was the most jealous woman in the kingdom .... At the time with the Jesuits, the dauphin was kept under close surveillance by his wife. He had wanted to show his inclination for the Marquise de Belsunce, as pretty as an angel; he had also favored the Marquise de Tessé, née de Noailles, a woman born to please; but his opening gambits had been quickly thwarted by the dauphine. Invited on several occasions to his chamber when he asked me to explain certain matters to him, I was well-placed to judge how things stood. I would see the dauphine seated in front of a loom working at the tambour in a tiny room with one small casement, which the dauphin turned into his library. His desk was covered with the best books which changed every week."

DUFORT DE CHEVERNY, *Mémoires sur les règnes de Louis XV et Louis XVI et sur la Révolution*, 1886.

In the seventeenth century, the dauphin's library and the private *cabinet intérieur* of the dauphine constituted a single space. Split into two in 1747, it had formerly been the bedchamber, first of Monseigneur, son of Louis XIV, and then of the dauphin, son of Louis XV, prior to his marriage.

Far from the ceremonial rooms, these two chambers communicated, making it possible for the young couple to benefit from a degree of intimacy that etiquette otherwise rendered impossible. Hugely fond of one another, the dauphin and dauphine would make sure to leave the door between the two rooms ajar.

FACING PAGE The library of the dauphin, son of Louis XV, served him at once as a place of work and as a retreat: more than merely observant, the heir to the French crown was pious, not to say monkish. The flap-top bureau in the center was supplied in 1756.

FACING PAGE Delivered in 1750, a cartel clock by the maker Martin of Paris,
in green-stained horn, stands in front of a pier glass in the dauphine's *cabinet intérieur*.
ABOVE Wonderfully framed against the wood paneling, *Autumn*, one of the Four Seasons
painted by Jean-Baptiste Oudry for this room in 1749.

FACING PAGE View of the dauphine's *cabinet intérieur*. The wooden panels are coated in
vernis Martin, a varnish that has something like the sheen of Japanese lacquer.
ABOVE Among the furniture is a chest of drawers by Gaudreaux and a sloped front desk signed by the famous
cabinetmaker Bernard Van Risen Burgh. These pieces, carried out for the first dauphine, Maria Teresa Rafaela,
were reemployed in 1747 for the dauphin's second wife, Maria Josepha of Saxony (1731–1767).

ABOVE Bed *à la polonaise* in the Dauphine's Bedchamber.
FACING PAGE A superb carpet with the French coat of arms, woven between 1760 and 1770.
It is rare for dyes in a rug to conserve so much of their original brightness and vigor.
Delivered at the end of the reign of Louis XV to Fontainebleau, it was acquired by Versailles in 2008.

The History GALLERIES

In 1830, when the Bourbons were definitively deposed from the throne of France, the fate of the château stood on a knife-edge. Some demanded it should be razed to the ground, while others lobbied for it to be converted into a school for agriculture. In 1833, Louis-Philippe, King of the French, took the decision to save Versailles and turn it into a museum of national history dedicated to "all the glories of France." So it was that, on June 10, 1837, the Citizen-King inaugurated the first galleries in the new Museum of French History.

FACING PAGE Full-length portrait of Louis-Philippe by François Xavier Winterhalter (1841).
The King of the French is represented in the Gallery of Battles, the centerpiece of the Museum
of French History, which he opened in 1837.

"This Hall [of 1792] is where modern military glory began…; it is a truly regal idea to represent the illustrious combatants of 1792 who were later to become kings simply wearing uniform. Who, walking through Hall of 1792, can dare despair of the future? This is the noblest and most eloquent lesson France could ever have learned for herself, and it will do her honor."

JEAN VATOUT, *Le Palais de Versailles*, 1837.

FACING PAGE View of the Hall of 1792 decorated with portraits of the generals who had distinguished themselves in action that year, starting with Louis-Philippe himself, represented as a lieutenant-general by Cogniet. The king did indeed serve in the Army of the Revolution under General Dumouriez, in which capacity he took part in the battles of Valmy and Jemmapes that famous year. During the Restoration, he commissioned Horace Vernet to paint a depiction of both these encounters. These compositions amount to pure propaganda, the aim being to present both battles as Louis-Philippe's personal victories. The function of the decoration in the Hall of 1792 is thus to highlight the revolutionary and republican credentials of the king, sole guarantor of genuine constitutional sovereignty, as stipulated in the charter of 1830.

PAGE 180 The Marquis de La Fayette by Court. The "hero of two worlds," who made a name for himself at the time of the War of American Independence (1775–1783), consolidating his reputation during the first two years of the French Revolution, played a far less glowing military role in 1792. Arraigned by the Assembly on August 10, 1792, he was declared a traitor to the nation a few days later. Forsaking his army, he then went over to the enemy. His presence in the Hall of 1792 is perhaps explained by the crucial support he provided at the time of the Revolution to the Duke of Orléans, who went on to be proclaimed King of the French as Louis-Philippe I.

PAGE 181 Above the door, Napoleon Bonaparte as a lieutenant-colonel in the first Corsican battalion in 1792, by Philippoteaux.

"What Louis-Philippe did in Versailles is good.
To have achieved this task is to show oneself great
as a king and impartial like a philosopher,
it is to have made a national monument out of a regal
monument, it is to have turned an immense idea
into an immense building, it is to have set up
the present in the past by confronting 1789 with 1688,
Emperor with King, Napoleon with Louis XIV;
in a word, it is to have given the magnificent book called
French history a magnificent binding called Versailles."

VICTOR HUGO, *Feuilles paginées III*, 1834–1837.

FACING PAGE
View of the Queen's Staircase from the Coronation Room.

"At the time of your last visit to Versailles,
Sire, you condescended to expound, before those
accompanying you, the plan you had formulated.
You told us how, without divesting the Louvre of its collections
of masterpieces of painting and sculpture and of old and
modern objets d'art that the Crown possesses there today,
you desire that Versailles present to France a gathering
of memorials of her history, and that monuments
to all the glories of the nation be deposited there and duly
displayed amid the magnificence of Louis XIV."

☒

Copy of a report to the king by Camille de Montalivet, intendant-general for the civil list,
and sanctioned by **LOUIS-PHILIPPE** on September 1, 1833.

FACING PAGE A detail of *Battle of Aboukir, 25 July 1799*
by Antoine-Jean Gros, hanging in the Coronation Room.

A "Gallery of Battles" was envisaged from the very start of the project to set up a museum of French history in 1833. In its final version, inaugurated on June 10, 1837, and preserved intact, the Gallery of Battles included some thirty-three pictures.

The first represents the battle of Tolbiac, won by Clovis in 711; the last, Wagram, shows the victory of Napoleon over the Austrians in 1809. All illustrate battles or events immediately before or after the actual engagement.

Apart from four, all the pictures were commissioned by Louis-Philippe. Thus, the scenes were far from randomly selected. Even more than the royal will, they constitute the translation of a political program intended to show the continuity between the two Frances—that before 1789 and the one which emerged from the Revolution—by way of an overarching and triumphant military epic.

Montalivet, intendant of the civil list to the king, explained some of the principles behind Louis-Philippe's choices: "He wanted the figures to be exactly those of the era the painter was called upon to recall; he desired the material representation of the facts to be as true to life as the history."

FACING PAGE View of the Gallery of Battles from the entrance.
PAGE 188 Detail of the vaulted dome over the gallery, showing a medallion
struck with an "L" and a "P," the initials of Louis-Philippe.
PAGE 189 View of the Gallery of Battles from the central colonnade.
The busts show military leaders who left an enduring stamp on French history.

"The July government, which had invited so many people to the entertainments at Versailles, neglected to convene those to whom it owes its existence and fortune…. A craving for command, empty platitudes, vainglorious predictions were not absent either from the festivities of the Republican era, nor from the solemnities of the Empire, nor from the anniversaries of the Restoration, and yet, none of these various regimes gained thereby one single extra hour of existence."

Le Siècle, June 16, 1837.

FACING PAGE Detail of a painting by Jean Alaux, *Valenciennes Taken by Storm, 1677*, 1837. In the foreground, a bust of Jean Baptiste Budes, Comte de Guébriant, marshal of France (1602–1643), by Cortot.

VALENCIENNES PRIS D'AS
PAR LE ROI (LOUIS XIV
17 Mai 1677.

*I*n 1095, at the time of the Council of Clermont, Pope Urban II proclaimed a crusade, exhorting the knights of the kingdoms of the West to conquer the Holy Land and take Jerusalem, the cradle of Christianity. This first crusade was completed four years later with the capture of the Holy City and the creation of the Latin States in the east.

From the twelfth to the end of the thirteenth century, the Christians of the West organized seven further campaigns. Though the eighth ended in 1272, this did not signal the end of the crusading ideal that lingered on into the fifteenth century.

Over time, a historiography of the crusades gradually grew up. The century of Louis XIV proved crucial to the construction of crusader history, with, for example, the *Histoire des croisades pour la délivrance de la Terre sainte* by Father Louis Maimbourg, published in 1675–1676. If the century of the Enlightenment placed something of an embargo on the subject, its fortunes improved at the beginning of the nineteenth century, when a novel, *Mathilde*, set during the third crusade, was published to great acclaim. A number of historians followed the trend and much light was cast on the phenomenon. Joseph Michaud, for instance, embarked on a monumental *Histoire des croisades*, the sixth edition of which had already appeared in 1841.

The Crusades Rooms in Louis-Philippe's Museum of French History issue from this cultural context and coincide with the king's political aim of reconciling those legitimists who remained faithful to the unseated Bourbons. A considerable number of them descended from families of ancient lineage who took part in the crusades.

FACING PAGE At the top left is Odier's painting of Eustace of Boulogne, brother of Godfrey of Bouillon, first sovereign of Jerusalem after it was captured by the crusaders. This is followed by depictions of the taking of Beirut in 1110 and the victory of Baldwin I, first titled king of Jerusalem (from 1100 to 1118). Below it are depictions of the capture of Beirut in 1109, and the battle of Jaffa, won in 1102 by Baldwin I, the first King of Jerusalem (1100–1118). On the right can be seen part of Victor Schnetz's *Battle of Ascalon* on August 12, 1099, in the course of which the Frankish army triumphed over an Egyptian force dispatched to recapture Jerusalem. PAGES 194-95 Detail of the ceiling decorated with armorial bearings of various noble families who fought in the crusades.

GAUTIER DE VIGNORY. HUGUES DE BEAUMEZ. MILON DE BRÉBAN, SEIGNEUR DE PROVINS. PHILIPPE DE CAULAINCOURT. GUILLAUME DE STRATEN. OTBERT DE ROUBAIX. GUILLAUME DE BAUDERRY.

EUSTACHE III
COMTE DE BOULOGNE __ ♦ 1125.

PRISE DE BARUTH
(17 Mai 1109)

COMBAT DE JAFFA
(1102)

PAR M. SERRUR.

1090 1147

RAYMOND V.
COMTE DE TOULOUSE.

LOUIS VII LE JEUNE.

Croisades

Croisades

GUILLAUME DE CHARTRES
GRAND-MAÎTRE de l'ORDRE du TEMPLE.
1217.

GIRARD DE LÉZAY.
1240.

GEOFFROY LE RATH.
G.MAÎTRE de l'ORDRE de S.JEAN de JÉRUSALEM.
1204.

ADAM DE SARCUS.
1240.

GILLES DE LANDAS.
1202.

GUILLAUME DE MESSEY.
1240.

HERVÉ CHRÉ

1248

GUILLAUME DE KERGARIOU

FACING PAGE AND ABOVE Sixteenth-century sculpture of Philippe de Villiers de l'Isle-Adam (1464–1534), forty-fourth Grand Master of the Order of Malta. Prior to the Revolution, it had been on display in the priory of the Temple in Paris. Behind the Grand Master, a detail of *The Lifting of the Siege of Malta Besieged by the Ottoman General Mustapha in September 1565* by Larivière, dating from 1842.

The Royal
OPERA

Debated from the time the court was first installed in Versailles by Louis XIV in 1682,
the construction of the Royal Opera only began at the end of the reign of Louis XV.
The king, who had long recoiled before the expense it entailed, was at last hustled across this particular
Rubicon by the impending weddings of his grandchildren, the contract for the building
being awarded to the architect Ange-Jacques Gabriel. The Opera House was inaugurated on May 16, 1770,
the day of the regal festivities celebrating the nuptials between the dauphin, Louis,
and Archduchess Marie-Antoinette.

FACING PAGE The façade of the Opera looks over the reservoir situated beyond the northern
wing of the château. The end range can be seen in the background to the right.

"I went to have a look at the new playhouse that required such a multitude of workmen to complete. It did much honor to M. Gabriel, and is the first building I ever saw so universally praised. It was of a form more elegant than is customary, with a great wealth and beauty of detail, both in the ornaments and the whole, and the embellishments my son pointed out to me appeared quite admirable. The height and depth above and below the house were dizzying, as were the particularities of the 'machines.' They made it a superb venue for festive entertainments, as it could be used for any purpose. It all must have been prodigiously costly, but no one could say how much."

DUC DE CROŸ, *Journal inédit*, April 22, 1770.

FACING PAGE The ceiling in the Royal Opera commissioned in 1768 from the painter
Louis Jacques Durameau and representing *Apollo Crowning the Arts*.
PAGES 202-3 View from the boxes to the stage showing a proscenium with the impressive dimensions of slightly
more than forty-three feet (thirteen meters) wide by nearly thirty-six feet (eleven meters) high.
The stage itself presents a surface area of 8,000 square feet (740 m²), which, until the inauguration
of the Palais Garnier in 1875, made the Royal Opera one of the largest auditoriums in Europe.

ABOVE AND FACING PAGE In accordance with the demands of Louis XV, Gabriel had to abandon his initial idea of a ceremonial box surmounted by a baldachin. Desirous of preserving his privacy, the king ordered his architect to set up a loggia protected by a grille instead. Though the original grille by the metal sculptor Roche has disappeared, a replica was made in 1957. The arabesque decorations on the box were executed by Louis Vernet to designs by the architect Charles de Wailly. PAGES 206–7 View from the stage into the house with carved decorations executed by Augustin Pajou. In line with the stage to the rear and beneath an apse-shaped exedra stands the royal box that Gabriel, acceding to the king's request, opted not to install in the recess provided.

FACING PAGE View of the loggia that swells out from the colonnade. Breaking the monotony, this architectural
device confers on the royal box a majestic grandeur unparalleled in any other European theater.
TOP, LEFT The cipher of the king, two intertwined "L's (for "Louis") surmounted by a crown.
TOP, RIGHT View on the box with the grille and the entrance to the amphitheatre. BOTTOM, LEFT The royal coat of arms in stone board by Pajou.
BOTTOM, RIGHT One of the fourteen Muses decorating the balustrade in front of the boxes in the stalls circle.

"A nation possessed the finest theater in the world....
But this glorious order, these adornments and ornaments,
all that which appeared so delightful to the public,
were less admirable than what could not be seen and
what could only be enjoyed through the effect created:
the wings, the flats, all that went unseen in the theater of which
I speak were the grandest and best-equipped imaginable.
For, is it not what happens behind the scenes at a theater that is
the focus of those recollections, intentions, and unspoken
motivations that only become consciousness and action
once the play takes place on stage? Those perspectives,
where astonishing sets conspired with unexpected entrances,
those heights whence Deities and liberating Powers would
descend for the denouement, the hell from which demons
and monsters emerged to belch out flames as from a furnace
and swallow up palaces, traitors, and ghosts alike,
were all grander here than anywhere else."

PAUL VALÉRY quoted by André Japy, *L'Opéra royal de Versailles*, 1958.

FACING PAGE View of King's private room, located on the same level as the royal box.
PAGE 210 The upper gallery leads to the Opera foyer.
PAGE 211 View of one of the staircases serving the various levels of the theater.

THE STABLES

On the eve of the Revolution, the stables of the king and their dependences boasted some 2,250 horses. The Great Stables were erected by Jules Hardouin-Mansart in 1679–1680 and today house the Carriage Museum, whose collections were amassed by Louis-Philippe and include vehicles of historical interest from the old civil list: the berlines used at the wedding of Napoleon I, Louis XVIII's hearse, the carriage employed for the coronation of Charles X, and so on.

FACING PAGE Inside the Great Stables, the headquarters since 2003
of the Equestrian Academy of Versailles, founded by Bartabas.
PAGE 216 The sleighs, *La Sirène* and *Les Roseaux*, were made in France c. 1740.
PAGE 217 The French coat of arms on the "Maison du Roi"
sedan chair dating from the second half of the eighteenth century.

ABOVE AND FACING PAGE Carriage used for the coronation of Charles X in Reims in 1825.
It was restored and altered in 1853 for Napoleon III, as indicated by the imperial eagle on the sides
and the medallion on top with the monogrammed N.

"On the night of June 3rd a truly daring robbery took place in the Great Stables at Versailles. The king being in Versailles, all the horse-blankets and caparisons were carried off; they must have been worth more than fifty thousand *écus*; the thieves took such precautions that, in so busy a household, no one realized anything was amiss, and in a single brief night the place was left bare without a soul being any the wiser. M. le Grand [Duke of Armagnac, and Master of the Royal Horse] entered in a fury, and all his subordinates besides. People were dispatched in every direction, Paris and Versailles were searched, but all to no avail."

SAINT-SIMON, *Mémoires*, 1699.

FACING PAGE Over the entrance porch to the Small Stables are three startlingly life-like horses, carved in the seventeenth century by Louis Le Conte. Today, the Small Stables host, among other things, a private gallery displaying some five thousand sculptures and casts.

THE GARDENS
of the Château

The beds, borders, and groves of Versailles occupy nearly two hundred acres (eighty hectares)
and are decorated with more than 450 carvings, statues, vases, and group sculptures, turning the gardens
into a vast museum of open-air sculpture. A further notable originality of the gardens
at Versailles is the ingenious water system comprising twenty-two miles (thirty-five kilometers)
of pipes that supply fifty-five fountains and almost six hundred water features.

FACING PAGE At the request of Louis XV, the *Salon Frais* (Cool Salon) was built
in the gardens of the Petit Trianon by Ange-Jacques Gabriel.
PAGES 224-25 View of part of the South Parterre, recognizable from
the embroidery-like pattern of boxwood shrubs.

FACING PAGE The rocaille ballroom, embellished with gilt-lead torches, was laid out by Le Nôtre in the early 1680s. ABOVE Bathed by their two eponymous basins, the walks (*allées*) of Bacchus and Saturn lead to groves in the garden's southern plantings. Bacchus, the god of wine and drunkenness, symbolizes autumn. In this gilt-lead group carved by the Marsy brothers, Bacchus is accompanied by satyrs, half-children, half-goats.

> "Then one should proceed straight above
> to the Latona basin, and pause to consider her,
> together with the lizards, the stairs, the statues,
> the Royal Walk, Apollo [and] the canal,
> before turning round to look at the plantings
> and the château."

LOUIS XIV

The elaborately carved group of the Basin of Latona (pages 230–231) recounts a tale from Ovid's *Metamorphoses* with deep roots in Ancient Greek mythology. Latona and her children, Diana and Apollo, are in Lycia, a region in ancient Greece located south of what is today Turkey. Waylaid and insulted by some country people, Latona seeks to protect her children and calls on divine vengeance. Jupiter harks to his lover's cries and promptly transforms the impious peasants into frogs and lizards. At the outset in 1670, the central group in marble, representing Latona and her children by the Marsy brothers, was set on a rock and the goddess looked out towards the château. The basin was altered between 1687 and 1689: placed on a circular base, Latona and her offspring now gaze down on Grand Canal. Some have analyzed the reuse of the story as an allusion to the disorders that marred the early years of Louis XIV's reign, a period known as the Fronde. In this reading, Latona would stand for the king's mother, the then regent, Anne of Austria, and the peasants transformed into amphibians and reptiles would represent the rebellious subjects duly punished.

FACING PAGE Bronze statues set about the rim of two rectangular basins in the Water Parterre.
Here the southern pool is decorated with a figure of Love flanked by two children.
PAGES 230-31 From the staircase leading to the Basin of Latona a fine perspective on the château opens out.
Leading far beyond the Royal Walk, the Basin of Apollo, and the Grand Canal,
it seems to encompass the whole horizon.

228

FACING PAGE Detail of the Colonnade, the vast marble peristyle measuring a hundred feet
(thirty-two meters) in diameter, erected by Jules Hardouin-Mansart (from 1685).
ABOVE A copy of the group *The Rape of Proserpine by Pluto*,
completed by François Girardon in 1699. The statue is a symbol of fire.

" It is as well to note at the outset that, as the Sun
is the emblem of the king, and poets equate the Sun
to Apollo, there is nothing in this superb abode
unconnected to this divinity; thus, none of the figures
and ornaments present have been placed by chance,
and all relate either to their location or to the Sun."

ANDRÉ FÉLIBIEN, *Description sommaire du château de Versailles, en 1674,*
in *Recueil des descriptions des peintures et autres ouvrages faits pour le Roi,*
chez la veuve de Sébastien Mâbre-Cramoisy, Paris, 1689.

PAGES 234-35 Work on the grotto at the Apollo baths began in 1776, after plans by Hubert Robert.
Entirely manmade, it was built in dressed stone by the contractor Thévenin.
FACING PAGE Detail of *Apollo Served by the Nymphs of Thetis,* a group carved by Girardon and Regnaudin, and erected in 1776
in the grotto at the Apollo baths. Originally, this group was commissioned to adorn the grotto of Thetys. Delivered in 1676,
it was set up eight years later to the rear of the garden, after Louis XIV had ordered the grotto to be demolished.
PAGES 238 AND 239 Reconstruction of the arbor around the perimeter of the Basin of Enceladus.

THE ORANGERY
of the Château

Versailles possessed an earlier orangery, built in 1663 by François Le Vau, but it did not survive the alterations made to the north-south axis of the gardens. Destroyed in 1681, it was replaced by a new plant house erected by Jules Hardouin-Mansart between 1683 and 1687. In its time, its dimensions were without equal in France or indeed in Europe.

FACING PAGE Planted in tubs, the shrubs (including orange, lemon, myrtle, and pomegranate trees) are brought into the Orangery in wintertime to protect them from frost.
PAGES 242-43 View down the arcade in the Orangery.

FACING PAGE AND ABOVE *Pluto Abducting Persephone* by François Girardon.
This sculpture was one of Girardon's masterpieces and was part of the "grand order" that Louis XIV
placed with a number of artists to provide decorative artworks for the grounds of Versailles.

*L*ike Le Vau's earlier building, Hardouin-Mansart's orangery leans against a slope. Both constructions were thus characterized by an original architectural principle: a gallery buttressed by two wings set at right angles. The dimensions of the second orangery are impressive: 500 feet (155 meters) long by 40 feet (12 meters) deep for the gallery, with wings 375 feet (114 meters) long. As for the arched ceiling, it reaches a height of 42 feet (13 meters). Hardouin-Mansart's monumental building is also remarkable for its unfussy ornamentation and masterful stone-dressing.

An architectural masterwork it may be, but the Orangery also has an important function to perform: to ensure that all the plants are safely protected from the winter chill. Hence its half-buried, solid stone construction sheltered from the cold north and east winds, warmed by the noonday sun through generous floor-to-ceiling windows. Walls varying between 4 and 5 meters thick mean that the temperature remains stable at 41–46°F (5–8°C), though to fully protect the shrubs it is still necessary to heat the building.

FACING PAGE At one end of the long gallery a stone niche hosts the statue of Louis XIV by Bernini.
Its story is worth telling. In June 1665, the Italian artist Gian Lorenzo Bernini arrived in Paris on the invitation of Louis XIV.
A multi-talented painter, sculptor, and architect, he was renowned throughout Europe. The king had called
on his services to complete the Louvre, in particular to draw up plans for the façade toward the church of Saint-Germain-
l'Auxerrois. In the end, Bernini's project for a colonnade was passed over and preference was given to designs by Charles Perrault,
a French architect backed by Colbert, who was appointed superintendent of the king's works in 1664.
However, Bernini's stay in Paris lived on, not only in a contemporary journal concerning the Cavalier Bernin
by Paul Fréart de Chantelou, but also in a bust of Louis XIV at the age of twenty-seven and an equestrian statue
of the king. Probably ordered from Bernini by Colbert in about 1665 to be erected in the space separating the Louvre
from the Tuileries, it languished in the artist's workshop in Rome until Bernini's death in 1680.
The masterpiece finally made its way to France in 1685, where Louis XIV came across it in Versailles.
Greatly displeased, the king ordered the sculptor François Girardon to make alterations and then
banished it to a corner beyond the Lake of the Swiss Guards. Thus the statue no longer represents the king
in antique garb, but the Roman Martius Curtius riding into the abyss to save the fatherland.

"I noticed again how, instead of going to see
his fountains and thus make a change to his walk,
he [Louis XIV]—as he always did in these gardens—would
just proceed back and forth along the balustrade
before the orangery, whence, on returning to the château,
he could see the quarters of the superintendence
where Louvois had just died [in 1691]. They terminated
the old wing of the château to the side of the orangery,
and the King kept his eyes fixed on them his
whole way back to the palace."

SAINT-SIMON, *Mémoires*, 1715.

FACING PAGE On fine days, the plants in tubs are taken out to join topiary trimmed into geometrical shapes.
PAGES 248–49 View of the Orangery parterre that in summer is adorned with bushes in tubs.
Beyond, the Lake of the Swiss Guards—so named as it was dug for the most part by members
of that regiment—today no longer forms part of the château, being separated from it by the Saint-Cyr road.

"Still, the Versailles of Louis XIV, this ruinous
and distateful masterpiece where changes
to the basins and arbors have sunk so much gold—though
it is hard to see where—could never have been finished.
Among the countless rooms piled one upon the other,
there is neither playhouse, nor banqueting room,
nor ballroom, and, to both front and rear, there remains
much to be done."

SAINT-SIMON, *Mémoires*, 1715.

FACING PAGE The parterre of the Orangery in the snow.

THE GRAND
Trianon

Ordained by Louis XIV in 1687, today's "Grand" Trianon replaces the earlier "Porcelain" Trianon,
so called because of its china decor. The new Trianon was from the start renowned for the beauty of its gardens.
Louis XV commissioned new buildings for the domain, including the Petit Trianon that Louis XVI
bestowed on Marie-Antoinette. Nineteenth-century opinion looked on the Trianon Palace more favorably
than on the rest of Versailles. Napoleon would reside there on imperial vacations and, after an eclipse
during the Restoration (1814–1830), Louis-Philippe and his family stayed there regularly.

FACING PAGE This columnated hall opens on to the reception apartment in the Grand Trianon,
with rooms whose names still resound to the entertainments of which
Louis XIV was so fond; the Music Room, the *Salon Frais*, the anteroom for games, and so on.

FACING PAGE The mirror-glass decoration set in the paneling was designed for Louis XIV and earned the room its current name of Mirror Room. The king turned the salon into a great room (*grand cabinet*), where he would convene his council whenever he was staying in the Trianon. The elegant sobriety of the wood carving on the walls is in keeping with the decoration in Queen Marie-Amélie's Bedchamber. Part of the furniture was made by Jacob-Desmalter for Empress Marie-Louise who had the room converted into a study.

ABOVE Detail on the base of one of the flambeaus in the Mirror Room, a copy of an example from the Emperor's great room in the Tuileries, and made in the 1960s. It was at that time that General de Gaulle decided to convert the Trianon into a residence for visiting sovereigns and foreign heads of state.

ABOVE Queen Marie-Amélie's Bedchamber was designed for Josephine, who never in fact went to the Trianon.
Only Empress Marie-Louise, whom Napoleon married in 1810, ever actually stayed in it. The balustrade was made for the Empress.
FACING PAGE The bed in Queen Marie-Amélie's Bedchamber speaks volumes as to the vicissitudes of French history
in the first half of the nineteenth century. It comes from the Tuileries, where it had been delivered for Napoleon in 1809,
and was later used by Louis XVIII when he resided in the Tuileries, the then seat of the restored royal regime.
After the king died there on September 16, 1824, Louis-Philippe, King of the French from 1830 to 1848, had it moved to the former
Empress's Bedchamber for his wife, Queen Marie-Amélie. Even the headboard bears the traces of successive political regimes.
If the palmettes and florets crowning the medallion date to the period of the Emperor (1804–1814), the cornucopias and rinceaus were created
for Louis XVIII (1814–1824), as was the crown, modified from the imperial to the royal type. The reign of Louis-Philippe ushered in further
alterations: his cypher of an interlaced "L" and "P" were added in the center of the medallion and the insignia of the Order of St. Michael
and the Order of the Holy Spirit of Louis XVIII were hammered out and replaced by other motifs such as the floral crown.

ABOVE The dressing table delivered in 1809 by Baudouin for Queen Marie-Amélie's Bedchamber was never used by Josephine, but only by Marie-Louise, daughter of the Emperor of Austria, unceremoniously married off to the man she had been brought up to detest. The chair dates to Louis-Philippe and the paneling to Louis XIV. Originally, they were to have been gilded, but the endless wars late in the reign of the Sun King made this impossible. Though unintentional, their simplicity nonetheless testifies to the change of taste and style signaled by the end of the reign of Louis XIV, of which the Royal Chapel offers a consummate illustration.

FACING PAGE This chest by the cabinetmaker Werner attracted notice in 1819 during an "exhibition of the products of industry." It was installed in the bedchamber for Queen Marie-Amélie. The vase in Sèvres porcelain shows Napoleon walking in the gardens of the palace of Sans-Souci, the property of King Frederick II of Prussia (1712–1786), which the Emperor of the French very much admired.

FACING PAGE The bedchamber in the apartment of the sovereign, featuring a pair of Sèvres vases from the period of Napoleon III standing on Masson's console table.
ABOVE Detail of the *commode* placed in the bedchamber of the apartment of the sovereign, improperly called the room of the Queen of the Belgians, for whom it was never destined. The console by Masson draws inspiration from the style of the foremost cabinetmaker of the age of Louis XIV, André-Charles Boulle.

FACING PAGE Detail of the circular table on display in the *Salon des Seigneurs* (Lords' Hall). The teak top measuring nine feet
(nearly three meters) across makes it one of the largest tables made in the Restoration period (1815–1830).
ABOVE Known as the Gallery of the Cotelles, this long-room contains twenty-one pictures painted
by Jean Cotelle. Forming a coherent cycle, they are devoted to views of the gardens of Versailles and the Trianon. All dating
from the late seventeenth century, they provide invaluable information as to the state of the gardens in the era of Louis XIV.
PAGES 264–65 This loggia, incorrectly dubbed a "peristyle," translates at once the talent of its architect, Jules Hardouin-Mansart, and
Louis XIV's royal will, though it is hard to say which came first. It was this elegant construction that earned
the Grand Trianon the sobriquet Château de Marbre. A seamless link between court and garden,
the near transparent screen confers on the château a feeling of buoyancy. Louis XIV saw the Grand Trianon
as a private retreat where he could withdraw with his family and escape the heavy hand of protocol.

THE PETIT
Trianon

*A masterpiece in the neoclassical style, the "Petit" Trianon was designed
by Ange-Jacques Gabriel between 1762 and 1769. Built as a place of leisure for Louis XV
on the initiative of Madame de Pompadour, she never lived to enjoy it as she died in 1764.
In 1774 Louis XVI presented the property to his wife with title deeds in the form of a pass-key
on a ribbon studded with 531 diamonds. Mindful of the memory of Marie-Antoinette,
whose presence here is more tangible than anywhere else in the palace, in 1867 Empress Eugenie
gathered together a small museum dedicated to the guillotined queen.*

FACING PAGE One of the armchairs in the reception room.

"Sometimes the queen would spend a month at a time in the Petit Trianon, where she had introduced all the customs of château life; when she entered her salon, neither would the ladies stop their piano or tapestrywork, nor the men halt their game of billiards or tric-trac [variant of backgammon].... The king and the princes would regularly go to supper there. The princesses' adornments were confined to a dress in white percale, a gauze fichu, and a straw hat."

MADAME CAMPAN, *Mémoires de Madame Campan,* first lady of the chamber to Marie-Antoinette.

FACING PAGE The splendid paneling in the Reception Room (Salon de Compagnie) was executed by Honoré Guibert for Louis XV, as shown by the medallions with the two intertwined "L"s of the royal cipher. The furniture is by Sené and the Foliot brothers. The fireside chairs and firescreen were delivered to the château at Saint-Hubert for Madame Du Barry in 1771. The lantern visible on the left is probably a piece by Thomire from about 1785, made at Marie-Antoinette's express request for this room. Sold off during the Revolution, it was purchased by Napoleon, though he was entirely unaware of the link between this lamp and the late queen.
PAGES 270 AND 271 A portrait of the Queen by Élisabeth Vigée-Lebrun known as *Marie-Antoinette with Rose*. This is one of the most famous likenesses of the unfortunate monarch. Unpretentiously portrayed in the gardens at the Petit Trianon and far from the pomp and rumors of the court, Marie-Antoinette appears at once unaffected and dignified.

"I have seen the enchanted desert,
Whose portrait is brushed by Taste;
I have seen the much-vaunted garden
Where Art, in imitating Nature, surpasses her....
Delightful Trianon, what diverse enthusiasms
You inspire to souls in love!
Entering beneath your verdant shades
I thought I espied the Isles of the Fortunate."

CHEVALIER BERTIN, *Les Jardins du Petit Trianon.*

FACING PAGE The windows of the Queen's Bedchamber open onto the Temple of Love
built by Mique in 1778. In the center stands a copy of Bouchardon's famous statue of 1750,
Love Carving his Bow out of Hercules' Club, placed there during the reign of Louis XVI.

FACING PAGE Detail of one of the chairs in the Queen's Bedchamber.

ABOVE The Queen's Bedchamber was furnished with unique rustic-style furniture of great originality recorded in documents as pieces "with Trelliswork" or "with Wheatears." Boasting carvings by Triquet and Rode, the ensemble was delivered to the queen by Georges Jacob in 1787 for her Bedchamber in the Petit Trianon. The wood is painted, as the craftsman noted himself in a memoir, "in the colors of truth and nature." The chair stiles terminate in pretty little pinecones and the garlanded wood carving is left unstained. By sheer luck, the original fabric showing a flower basin embroidered in Lyon by Desfarges survives. The fabric is a prime example of exactly the kind of embroidered fabrics the queen favored. By a bitter irony of history, the furniture was sold off in October 1793, a few days before Marie-Antoinette was executed. Part was bought back by Versailles (though not the imperial bed with drapes that is not original) in 1945.

"Its furnishings were characterized by elegance
rather than by magnificence, and many Paris
townhouses were more remarkable. The salon was
ornamented with paintings and the bedroom draped
in muslin whose embroidery and vivid coloring
vied with the most skillful brush. Some portraits
of Maria Theresa's children transported the queen
back to her family circle, where, with less grandeur,
she would have found greater happiness."

COMTE D'HÉZECQUES, *Souvenirs d'un page de la cour de Louis XVI*, 1873.

FACING PAGE The Queen's boudoir was especially created for Marie-Antoinette in 1776
and is the most intimate room in the Queen's Apartment at the Petit Trianon. The decoration dates from 1787.
To benefit from greater privacy, Marie-Antoinette commissioned a system of elevating mirrors
from Mercklein. Rising up from the basement, they form a double screen that protects
the room from prying eyes to the side leading to the precinct and to the garden front.
Mercklein's ingenious contraption was reinstated in 1985.

ABOVE AND FACING PAGE The tester bed *à la polonaise* in the King's Bedchamber dates to the eighteenth century, the posts being adorned with lion muzzles. It is covered with crimson and white lampas *à la musique chinoise*, with motifs showing chinoiserie minstrels, redolent of those on textiles delivered to Louis XV in 1768.

ABOVE Warding away unwelcome visitors, the Medusa's head adorning the main
staircase in the Petit Trianon was carved by Honoré Guibert at the end of the reign of Louis XV.
FACING PAGE The main staircase at the Petit Trianon was designed by Ange-Jacques Gabriel,
Louis XV's *premier architecte*. The neoclassical style ironwork forged by Brochois is especially remarkable.

THE GARDENS
of the Petit Trianon

Nestling within the gardens of the Petit Trianon stand three buildings whose modest size far from obscures their incomparable charm. Next to an artificial rock down which cascades a waterfall, the Belvedere or "Salon du Rocher" was built by Richard Mique in 1778. It gazes down on a small lake out of which flows a rivulet that meanders to the Temple of Love with its dome borne on twelve Corinthian columns. Finally, the French Pavilion, completed in 1750, is the work of Ange-Jacques Gabriel and bears witness to the rocaille style Louis XV did much to encourage.

PAGES 282-83 Each of the four façades of the Petit Trianon is visibly distinct.
In the design for the one that looks over the French garden, Ange-Jacques Gabriel provides a virtuoso reinterpretation of the style of the Italian Renaissance architect Andrea Palladio.
FACING PAGE The interior of the Belvedere is decorated with stucco painted with arabesques.

ABOVE The Belvedere, a pavilion decorated in the neoclassical style, was erected by Mique in 1778
for Marie-Antoinette. Its eight French windows are surmounted alternately by a pediment and a bas-relief.
The bas-reliefs illustrate the four seasons, while the pediments feature their attributes.
FACING PAGE The domed ceiling of the Belvedere, with a hanging lantern in the center.

Details of the painted walls of the Belvedere. The light-hearted, mischievous quality
of the scenes conveys the relaxed spirit associated with this structure.

FACING PAGE A detail of the sculpture by Bouchardon
(which is in fact a copy made by Mouchy in 1778–80) erected in the middle of the Temple of Love.
ABOVE The Temple of Love stands in the English-style garden planted
in keeping with Marie-Antoinette's taste.

"Is it not, however, quite natural that it appears agreeable to a sovereign, who is always on show and chained by the most rigorous etiquette, to be able to withdraw into some solitary abode to divest himself there of the burdens of grandeur?"

COMTE D'HÉZECQUES, *Souvenirs d'un page de la cour de Louis XVI*, 1873.

FACING PAGE The pavilion in the French garden, commonly called the French Pavilion, was built by Gabriel between 1749 and 1750 and is considered a model of rocaille architecture. Quite apart from the decoration on the walls, the floor in the reception room is composed of different varieties of marble: veined white, garnet marble from the Languedoc, Campan green, and so on.

DARDANUS

TRAGÉDIE LYRIQUE

En quatre Actes

Représentée pour la premiere fois devant leurs Majestés
à Triannon le 18 Septembre 1784. et par l'Académie
Royale de Musique le 30 novembre suivant.

MISE EN MUSIQUE

PAR

M.ʳ SACCHINI.

A PARIS

Ché's l'Auteur rue basse du Rempart N.º 17.
Ché's le S.ʳ Sieber rue S.ᵗ Honoré N.º 92
Et aux adresses ordinaires
A. P. D. R.
Gravée par G. Magnian rue S.ᵗ Honoré vis-à-vis la Barriere des Sergents

"The queen's notion of living in the Trianon, free of all formality, was followed by the idea of staging plays, as had by then become the custom almost everywhere in the countryside. It was agreed that, save for Monsieur le Comte d'Artois, no young man would be admitted to the troupe and that the sole spectators would be the king, Monsieur, and the princesses who did not perform; but, to encourage the actors a little, the stalls boxes would be occupied by the women who read to the queen, by her ladies-in-waiting, their sisters and daughters, making some forty people in all."

MADAME CAMPAN, *Mémoires de Madame Campan,* first lady of the chamber to Marie-Antoinette.

PAGE 294 *Dardanus*, a tragic opera in four acts by Sacchini,
was performed before the king and queen in the theater of the Trianon on September 18, 1784.
PAGE 295 AND FACING PAGE The Queen's Theater was erected in 1780 by Richard Mique. It is a private theater in the sense that the queen would invite only the royal family and close friends to performances. Its interior decoration is nonetheless elaborate, in particular the gilded pasteboard sculptures that emblazon the stage and hold up the ruched curtain.

$\mathcal{I}$nagurated on June 1, 1780, with a *Prologue to the Opening of the Theater at the Trianon* composed by Despréaux of the Royal Academy of Music, the Queen's Theater was erected by Richard Mique from 1778 to 1780, on the site of one of Louis XV's greenhouses. In keeping with the trend for private theaters, Marie-Antoinette set up a small company comprised of friends and even trod the boards herself. The debut production, Sedaine's *La Gageure imprévue*, opened on August 1, 1780.

ABOVE Detail on the vaulted ceiling in the Queen's Theater decorated with Marie-Antoinette's initials, an "M" entwined with an "A." FACING PAGE The ceiling is a copy of *Apollo, the Muses and the Graces* by Jean-Jacques Lagrenée carried out in the twentieth century.
PAGES 300-1 The French pavilion seen from the *jardin français* of the Petit Trianon.

The Queen's HAMLET

*Situated in the estate of the Trianon, the Queen's Hamlet (*Hameau de la Reine*)
was laid out by the architect Richard Mique between 1783 and 1785. Inspired by the villages of Normandy,
it is composed of modest thatched-roofed cottages scattered around a lake. Although the hamlet was very much part
of the fashion for a "return to nature," the queen was not simply content to play the shepherdess, but set up a real
farm directed by a real farmer who would regularly send produce to the château kitchens.*

FACING PAGE The Marlborough Tower (from the name of a song Madame Poitrine, the dauphin's wetnurse,
had brought back in fashion at the end of the eighteenth century) dominates the lake in the Queen's Hamlet.
Its base, partly hidden by vegetation, contains a fishing lodge. The cottage in the background houses the dairy.
PAGES 304-5 Gateway to the farm to the west end of the hamlet.

"One of the thatched cottages housed the dairy,
while the cream, contained in porcelain vases one atop
the other on white marble tables, was kept fresh
by a stream diverted through the room. Next door was
a real farm, where the queen bred a herd of superb Swiss
cattle that would graze in the surrounding meadows."

COMTE D'HÉZECQUES, *Souvenirs d'un page de la cour de Louis XVI*, 1873.

FACING PAGE Detail of the fountain at the dairy decorated with a goat's head.
PAGES 308 AND 309 Originally, the Queen's Hamlet possessed two dairies: one made the produce,
while the other was for cleaning and storing the containers. The first was pillaged during the Revolution
and then destroyed during the First Empire. PAGE 308 A view of the second dairy, restored
between 1811 and 1818. The grandiose marble table beneath the trompe-l'œil coffered ceiling is by Boichard.
Under the fountain and the window stand smaller tables, also in marble. Are they perhaps the ones
on which the queen would ask her staff to place the Sèvres china milk pots?
PAGE 309 Directly above one of the tables, a fountain installed in a niche. Two entwined
dolphins comprise the foot of the fountain.

ABOVE Waterlilies on the artificial lake specially dug for the Queen's Hamlet.
FACING PAGE An eighteenth-century bust of a young peasant.

"At the end of the Trianon gardens, the river
was bordered by an infinitude of thatched cottages which,
while appearing rustic from the outside, were
elegant and sometimes exquisite within. In the middle
of this little hamlet, a high tower, dubbed
the Marlborough Tower, dominated the surroundings.
Its outside staircase, adorned with gillyflowers
and geraniums, looked like a flowerbed in the air."

ℚ

COMTE D'HÉZECQUES, *Souvenirs d'un page de la cour de Louis XVI*, 1873.

FACING PAGE The mill in the Queen's Hamlet.
The wheel does not turn—its purpose is purely decorative.

Bibliography

STUDIES

Arizzoli-Clémentel, Pierre and Jean-Pierre Samoyault, *Le Mobilier de Versailles, Chef-d'œuvres du XIXe siècle*, Dijon: Faton, 2009.

Arizzoli-Clémentel, Pierre (gen. ed.), *Versailles*, Paris: Citadelles & Mazenod, 2009, 2 vols.

Arizzoli-Clémentel, Pierre, *Le Mobilier de Versailles: XVIIe et XVIIIe siècles*, Dijon: Faton, 2002, vol. 2.

Baulez, Christian, *Versailles, deux siècles d'histoire de l'art*, Versailles: Société des Amis de Versailles, 2007.

Baulez, Christian, *Visite du Petit Trianon et du hameau de la Reine*, Versailles: Artlys, 2007.

Deslot, Thierry, *Le Hameau de la Reine. Une journée avec Marie-Antoinette*, Levallois-Perret: Maé éditions, 2005.

Gady, Alexandre (gen. ed.), *Jules Hardouin-Mansart (1646–1708)*, Paris: Éd. de la Maison des Sciences de l'Homme, 2010.

Gaehtgens, Thomas W., "Le musée historique de Versailles," in Pierre Nora (gen. ed.), *Les Lieux de mémoire*, Paris: Gallimard, 1986, vol. 2, *La Nation*, part 3, *La gloire, les mots*, p. 143–168.

Gaehtgens, Thomas W., *Versailles, de la résidence royale au Musée historique*, Antwerp: Fonds Mercator, 1984.

Gousset, Jean-Paul and Raphaël Masson, *Versailles. L'Opéra royal*, Versailles: Château de Versailles/Artlys, 2010.

Himelfarb, Hélène, "Versailles, fonctions et legends" in Pierre Nora (gen. ed.), *Les Lieux de mémoire*, Paris, Gallimard, 1986, vol. 2. *La Nation*, part 2, *Le territoire, l'État, le patrimoine*, pp. 235–292 .

Jacquet, Nicolas, *Versailles secret et insolite*, Paris: Parigramme, 2011.

Japy, André, *L'Opéra royal de Versailles*, n.p.: Comité National pour la Sauvegarde du Château de Versailles, 1958.

Les Laques du Japon. Collections de Marie-Antoinette (exh. cat. by Monika Kopplin with an essay by Christian Baulez), Paris: RMN/Versailles, 2001.

Léonard-Roques, Véronique (gen. ed.), *Versailles dans la littérature. Mémoire et imaginaire aux XIXe et XXe siècles*, Clermont-Ferrand: PU Blaise Pascal, 2005.

Meyer, Daniel, *Le Mobilier de Versailles: XVIIe et XVIIIe siècles*, Dijon: Faton, 2002, vol. 1, *Les meubles royaux prestigieux*.

Newton, William Ritchey, *Derrière la façade. Vivre au château de Versailles au XVIIIe siècle*, Paris: Perrin, 2008.

Pérouse de Montclos, Jean-Michel, *Versailles*, New York: Abbeville, 1991.

Pommier, Édouard, "Versailles, l'image du souverain," in Pierre Nora (gen. ed.), *Les Lieux de mémoire*, Paris: Gallimard, 1986, vol. 2, *La Nation*, part 2, *Le territoire, l'État, le patrimoine*, pp. 193–234.

Rohan, Olivier de, Roland de L'Espée, and Jean-Marie Pérouse de Montclos, *Un siècle de mécénat à Versailles, Versailles*, Paris: Société des Amis de Versailles/ Éditions du Regard, 2007.

Sabatier, Gérard, *Versailles ou la figure du roi*, Paris: Albin Michel, 1999.

Saule, Béatrix, *Visiter Versailles*, Versailles: Artlys, 2006.

Saule, Béatrix, *Visite du musée des Carrosses*, Versailles: Artlys, 1997.

Sèvres-Cité de la Céramique and John Whitehead, *Sèvres sous Louis XVI et la Révolution: le premier apogée*, Paris: Éditions courtes et longues, 2010.

Whitehead, John, *Sèvres at the time of Louis XV. Birth of a Legend*, Paris: Éditions courtes et longues, 2010.

Soieries de Lyon: commandes royales au XVIIIe siècle, 1730–1800 (exh. cat. by Pierre Arizzoli-Clémentel and Chantal Gastinel-Coural), Musée Historique des Tissus, Lyon, 1988.

Verlet, Pierre, *Le Mobilier royal français*, Paris: Picard, 1990–1999, 4 vols (2nd ed.).

Verlet, Pierre, *French 18th-century Furniture*, Charlottesville: University of Virginia Press, 1991.

Verlet, Pierre, *Le Château de Versailles*, Paris: Fayard, 1985 (2nd ed.).

MEMOIRS, ACCOUNTS, LETTERS, ETC.

Boigne, Éléonor-Adèle d'Osmond, Countess of, *Mémoires de la comtesse de Boigne, née d'Osmond, récits d'une tante*, (ed. Jean-Claude Berchet), Paris: Mercure de France, 1999, 2 vols.

Memoirs of the Countess of Boigne (ed. Anka Muhlstein), New York: Turtle Point Press, 2004, 2 vols.

Madame Campan, *Mémoires de Madame Campan, première femme de chambre de Marie-Antoinette* (ed. Carlos de Angulo with a preface by Jean Chalon), Paris: Mercure de France, 1999.

Memoirs of Madame Campan on Marie Antoinette and her Court (tr. G. K. Fortescue), Charleston: Bibliobazaar, 2009.

Croÿ-Solre, Emmanuel de, Duke, *Journal inédit du duc de Croÿ (1718–1784)* (eds. Vicômte de Grouchy and Paul Cottin), Paris: Flammarion, 1906–1921, 4 vols.

Dufort de Cheverny, Jean-Nicolas, *Mémoires sur les règnes de Louis XV et Louis XVI et sur la Révolution* (ed. Robert de Crèvecœur), Paris: Plon, Nourrit et Cie, 1886, 2 vols.

Hézecques, Félix de France, Count, *Souvenirs d'un page de la cour de Louis XVI* (ed. Count d'Hézecques), Paris: Didier, 1873.

James, Henry, *The Portrait of a Lady,* London: Penguin, 2003.

Louis XIV, *Manière de montrer les jardins de Versailles* (ed. Simone Hoog), Paris: RMN, 2001.

Louis XIV, *The Way to Present the Gardens of Versailles* (ed. Simone Hoog), Paris: RMN, 2001.

Marie-Antoinette, *Correspondance, 1770–1793* (ed. Évelyne Lever), Paris: Tallandier, 2006.

Imperial Mother, Royal Daughter. The Correspondence between Marie Antoinette, and Maria Theresa, London: Sedgwick and Jackson, 1986.

Orleans, Charlotte Elizabeth of Bavaria, Duchess of, *Lettres de Madame, duchesse d'Orléans, née princesse Palatine* (ed. Olivier Amiel, with a preface by Pierre Gascar), Paris: Mercure de France, 1999.

Memoirs of the Princess Palatine, Princess of Bohemia, Including Her Correspondence with the Great Men of Her Day [...], (ed. Marie Pauline Rose Blaze de Bury), Delaware: Adamant Media Corporation, 2005.

Proust, Marcel, *À la recherche du temps perdu* (ed. Jean-Yves Tadié), Paris: Gallimard, 1987–1989, 4 vols.

Proust, Marcel, *In Search of Lost Time* (tr. C. Scott-Moncrieff, with S. Hudson), London: Bibliophile Editions, 2006, 3 vols.

Saint-Simon, Louis de Rouvroy, Duke, *Mémoires, 1691–1723*, ed. Yves Coirault, Paris, Gallimard, 1983–1988, 8 vols.

Saint-Simon, Louis de Rouvroy, Duke, *Memoirs of Louis XIV and Regency,* Charleston: Bibliobazaar, 2008, 10 vols.

Saint-Simon, Louis de Rouvroy, Duke, *Parallèle des trois premiers rois Bourbons* in *Traités politiques et autres écrits* (ed. Yves Coirault), Paris: Gallimard, 1996.

Quotation Sources

Page 8
Saint-Simon, *Mémoires, 1691–1723*, p. 522.

Page 23
Marcel Proust, *In Search of Lost Time. The Captive*, p. 776.

Page 32
Jean-Baptiste Colbert and King Louis XIV, quoted by Pierre Verlet, *Le Château de Versailles*, p. 98.

Page 39
Saint-Simon, *Mémoires, 1691–1723*, p. 618.

Page 40
Saint-Simon, *Mémoires, 1691–1723*, p. 36.

Page 46
Duc de Croÿ, *Journal inédit*, p. 397.

Page 58
Madame Campan, *Mémoires de Madame Campan, première femme de chambre de Marie-Antoinette*, p. 170.

Page 65
Saint-Simon, *Mémoires, 1691–1723*, p. 791.

Page 75
Duc de Croÿ, *Journal inédit*, p. 396.

Page 80
Madame Campan, *Mémoires de Madame Campan, première femme de chambre de Marie-Antoinette*, p. 90–91.

Page 86
Saint-Simon, *Mémoires, 1691–1723*, p. 605.

Page 89
Saint-Simon, *Mémoires, 1691–1723*, p. 463.

Page 113
Duc de Croÿ, *Journal inédit*, p. 71–72.

Page 121
Madame Campan, *Mémoires de Madame Campan, première femme de chambre de Marie-Antoinette*, p. 96.

Page 126
Madame Campan, *Mémoires de Madame Campan, première femme de chambre de Marie-Antoinette*, p. 133.

Page 129
Edmond and Jules de Goncourt, quoted by Thierry Deslot, *Le Hameau de la Reine. Une journée avec Marie-Antoinette*.

Page 136
Marie-Antoinette, *Correspondance, 1770–1793*, p. 115.

Page 142
Marie-Antoinette, *Correspondance, 1770–1793*, p. 225.

Page 151
Duc de Croÿ, *Journal inédit*, p. 228.

Page 160
Comte d'Hézecques, *Souvenirs d'un page de la cour de Louis XVI*, p. 107.

Page 168
Dufort de Cheverny, *Mémoires sur les règnes de Louis XV et Louis XVI et sur la Révolution*, p. 101–102.

Page 178
Jean Vatout, quoted by Thomas W. Gaehtgens, *Versailles, de la résidence royale au Musée historique*, p. 278.

Page 183
Victor Hugo quoted by Thomas W. Gaehtgens, *Le musée historique de Versailles*, p. 167.

Page 184
Camille de Montalivet, quoted by Thomas W. Gaehtgens, *Le musée historique de Versailles*, p. 148–149.

Page 190
Extract from *Le Siècle*, quoted by Thomas W. Gaehtgens, *Le musée historique de Versailles*, p. 167.

Page 200
Duc de Croÿ, *Journal inédit*, p. 390.

Page 211
Paul Valéry quoted by André Japy, *L'Opéra royal de Versailles*, p. 58–61.

Page 220
Saint-Simon, *Mémoires, 1691–1723*, p. 618.

Page 228
Louis XIV, *Manière de montrer les jardins de Versailles*, 2001.

Page 236
André Félibien, quoted by Jean-Pierre Néraudau, *L'Olympe du Roi-Soleil*, p. 195.

Page 246
Saint-Simon, *Mémoires, 1691–1723*, p. 495–496.

Page 251
Saint-Simon, *Mémoires, 1691–1723*, p. 533.

Page 268
Madame Campan, *Mémoires de Madame Campan, première femme de chambre de Marie-Antoinette*, p. 189–190.

Page 272
Chevalier Bertin, *Les Jardins du Petit Trianon*.

Page 276
Comte d'Hézecques, *Souvenirs d'un page de la cour de Louis XVI*, p. 240–241.

Page 292
Comte d'Hézecques, *Souvenirs d'un page de la cour de Louis XVI*, p. 238.

Page 297
Madame Campan, *Mémoires de Madame Campan, première femme de chambre de Marie-Antoinette*, p. 190.

Page 306
Comte d'Hézecques, *Souvenirs d'un page de la cour de Louis XVI*, p. 244.

Page 312
Comte d'Hézecques, *Souvenirs d'un page de la cour de Louis XVI*, p. 244.

Front flap
Henry James, *The Portrait of a Lady*, p. 270.

Index

A

Adélaïde, Madame, Daughter of France 114, 156
Alaux, Jean 190
Angoulême, Duke of, Louis Antoine d'Artois 151
Anne of Austria, Queen of France 228
Apollo Room 4, 35
Armagnac, Duke of, Louis de Lorraine 220
Artois, Comtesse d' (Marie Thérèse de Savoie) 142

B

Bartabas 214
Bathroom 23, 121, 122, 148, 151, 154, 155
Baudouin, Antoine-Thibaut 258
Beaumarchais, Pierre Augustin Caron de 114
Bedchamber of the apartment of the sovereign
    (also known as the room of the Queen of the Belgians) 261
Bedchamber of the Dauphin Louis 166
Bellan, Martin 73
Belsunce, Marquise de, Jeanne Edmée 168
Bernini, Gian Lorenzo 244
Bertin, Antoine 272
Billiard Room 40, 90
Bonaparte, Napoleon 178, 183, 187, 214, 218, 253, 256, 258, 268
Bouchardon, Edmé 272, 291
Bouillon, Godefroy of 192
Boulard, Jean Baptiste 151
Boulle, André-Charles 89, 261
Boulogne, Eustace of 192
Brochois, François 280
Brun, Louis Auguste 148
Budes, Jean Baptiste (Comte de Guébriant) 190
Bull's-eye Room (*Salon de l'Œil-de-bœuf*) 53, 78, 82

C

Caffiéri, family 94
Campan, Jeanne Louise Henriette Genet 56, 80, 126, 268, 297
Carriage Museum 214
Cartellier, Pierre 8
Cassette (Purse Room) 121, 122
Castries, Marquis de (Charles Eugène Gabriel) 151
Chantelou, Paul Fréart de 244
Charles IX, King of France 136
Charles X, Comte d'Artois and King of France 151, 214, 297
Châteauroux, Madame de (Marie Anne de Mailly) 156
Cheverny, Dufort de 168
Clicquot, Robert 73
Clotilde, Marie 140
Cogniet, Léon 178
Colbert, Jean-Baptiste 31, 32, 244
Corner Room 101, 156
Coronation Room 183
Cortot, Jean Pierre 190
Cotelle, Jean 263
Court, Joseph Désiré 178

Coustou, Guillaume 65
Coustou, Nicolas 85
Coypel, Antoine 65
Coysevox, Antoine 114, 214
Croÿ, Duc de (Emmanuel de Croÿ-Solre) 44, 75, 113, 151, 200
Crusades Room 192, 197

D

Daguerre, Dominique 131
Dauphine's Bedchamber 174
Dauphin's Library 168
Dauthiau, Louis 94
Degoullons, Jules 73
Dellalande, Michel-Richard 80
Delanois, Louis 160
Desfarges, Marie-Olivier 55, 275
Desjardins, Martin (born under the name Van den Bogaert) 18
Despréaux, Jean-Etienne 298
Didier, Frédéric 121
Domitian, Roman Emperor 43
Du Barry, Madame (Jeanne Bécu) 156, 160, 162, 268
Dumouriez, Charles-François 178
Durameau, Louis Jacques 200

E

Empress's Bedchamber 256, 258
Eugénie de Montijo, Empress consort of the French 267

F

Félibien, André 236
Foliot, brothers 93, 268
Fornaro, Duke of, (Ferdinand Colonna) 65
French Pavilion 286, 292, 298

G

Gabriel, Ange-Jacques 32, 198, 200, 204, 267, 280, 286, 292
Gallery of Battles 176, 187
Gallery of the Cotelles 263
Gaudreaux, Antoine 101, 106, 110, 173
Girardon, François 233, 236, 244
Gluck, Christoph Willibald 126
Gold Room (*Cabinet Doré*) 4, 126, 129, 131, 132
Goldoni, Carlo 114
Goncourt, Edmond et Jules de 129
Grand cabinet of Madame Du Barry 156
Grand Canal 44, 228
Grand Couvert 80
Grand Degré (or Gabriel Staircase) 32
Grand Trianon 253, 256, 263
Great Stables 214, 220
Grétry, André Ernest Modeste 126
Gros, Antoine-Jean 184
Guardroom 59
Guibert, Honoré 268, 280

H

Hall of Mirrors (*Galerie des Glaces*) 11, 18, 32, 35, 40, 44, 51, 78
Hardouin-Mansart, Jules 4, 31, 214, 233, 240, 244, 263
Hauré, Jean 56, 154
Henry III, King of France 136
Henry IV, King of France 136
Hézecques, Comte d' (Félix) 160, 276, 292, 306, 312
Hugo, Victor 15, 183, 184

J

Jacob-Desmalter, François-Honoré-Georges 255
Jacob, Georges 126, 142, 145, 275
Japy, André 211
Joséphine, Empress of France 256, 258
Joubert, Gilles 101, 110
Jouvenet, Jean 65

K

King's Apartment 53, 78, 85
King's Chamber 82, 85, 86, 89, 278
King's Petit Degré 27
King's Private Apartment (*Appartement Intérieur*) 4, 90, 110, 121
King's Room 85
King's Study (*Cabinet Intérieur*) 101, 102, 106, 110, 113
King's Suite (*Grand Appartement*) 35, 114

L

La Fayette, Marquis de (Gilbert du Motier) 178
La Fosse, Charles de 65
La Vallière, Madame de (Louise Françoise de la Baume-le-Blanc) 8
Lagrenée, Jean-Jacques 298
Lalande, Robert de 73
Larivière, Charles Philippe 197
Le Brun, Charles 32, 44
Le Goupil, André 73
Le Vau, François 31, 240, 244
Lecomte, Félix 51
Lécot, Jean François 132
Lemoyne, François 36
Leszczinska, Marie 51, 55, 124, 134
Levasseur, Étienne 94
L'Isle-Adam, Philippe de Villiers de 197
Loo, Louis Michel Van 166
Lords' Hall (*Salon des Seigneurs*) 263
Louis-Philippe, King of the French 8, 85, 148, 176, 178, 183, 187, 192, 214, 253, 256, 258
Louis Ferdinand de Bourbon, Dauphin Louis 166
Louis IX, Saint Louis, King of France 8, 68, 85
Louis XIII, King of France 8, 11, 18, 26
Louis XIV, King of France 4, 8, 11, 15, 18, 26, 31, 32, 35, 36, 43, 44, 60, 68, 78, 80, 85, 89, 90, 101, 124, 166, 168, 183, 184, 192, 198, 214, 228, 236, 244, 246, 251, 253, 255, 258, 261, 263
Louis XV, King of France 4, 8, 27, 32, 35, 51, 73, 90, 94, 98, 101, 102, 104, 110, 114, 121, 122, 124, 156, 164, 166, 168, 174, 198,
200, 204, 253, 267, 268, 278, 280, 286, 298
Louis XVI, King of France 23, 24, 44, 53, 56, 85, 89, 90, 92, 93, 94, 101, 110, 114, 116, 118, 122, 134, 140, 151, 154, 160, 166, 253, 267, 272, 276, 306, 312
Louis XVII, Dauphin of France 166
Louis XVIII, King of France 24, 89, 214, 256
Louise-Élisabeth of France (Duchess of Parma) 90
Louvois, Marquis de (François Michel le Tellier) 246
Lower Gallery 18
Ludwig II, King of Bavaria 32
Luynes, Duc de (Charles Philippe d'Albert) 101

M

Mâbre-Cramoisy, Sébastien 236
Madame de Pompadour's second anteroom 164
Madame Du Barry's Library 156
Madame Poitrine (Marie Madeleine Bocquet) 312
Maintenon, Madame de (Françoise d'Aubigné) 80, 89
Marble Court 11, 15, 35, 113, 160
Marble Hall 15, 18, 148
Maria Anna of Bavaria, Dauphine of France 51
Maria Christina, Archduchess of Austria 147
Maria Josepha of Saxony, Dauphine of France 134, 168, 173
Maria Teresa Rafaela, Infanta of Spain and Dauphine of France 166, 173
Maria Theresa of Austria, Queen of France 31, 51, 55, 114, 124, 276
Maria Theresa, Queen of Hungary and Croatia 131, 136, 142
Marie Adélaïde of Savoy, Dauphine of France 51
Marie-Amélie Thérèse de Bourbon, Queen of France 255, 256, 258
Marie-Antoinette, Queen of France 11, 44, 51, 53, 55, 56, 80, 85, 93, 101, 124, 126, 129, 131, 132, 134, 136, 139, 142, 147, 148, 198, 253, 267, 268, 275, 276, 288, 291, 297, 298
Marie-Antoinette's Private Rooms 124, 126
Marie-Louise of Austria, Empress of France 218, 255, 256, 258
Martin, brothers 171
Maurepas, Marquis de (Jean Frédéric Phélypeaux) 151
Mazarin, Jules 11, 43
Mercklein, Jean Tobie 276
Mercury Room 35
Metz, Marquis de 65
Mique, Richard 126, 272, 286, 288, 297, 298, 302
Mirror Room 255
Montalivet, Camille de 184, 187
Mouchy, Louis Philippe 291
Mozart, Wolfgang Amadeus 73, 114
Mustapha Pacha, Lala 197

N

Nadermann, Jean Henri 129
Napoleon III, Emperor of the French 261
Nattier, Jean-Marc 90, 164
Necker, Jacques 151
Normandy, Duke of (Louis Charles) 145

O

Œben, Jean François 102
Odier, Édouard 192
Orangery 240, 244, 246, 251
Orbay, François d' 31
Orléans, Philippe d' 65
Oudry, Jean-Baptiste 124, 171

P

Pajou, Augustin 162, 204, 209
Palladio, Andrea 286
Parrocel, Joseph 80
Passemant, Claude Siméon 94
Peace Room 40
Petit Trianon 253, 267, 268, 272, 275, 276, 280, 286, 297
Petitot, Louis 8
Philippoteaux, Félix 178
Place d'Armes 8
Poets' Room 134
Polignac, Duchesse de (Yolande de Polastron) 151
Pompadour, Marquise de (Jeanne Antoinette Poisson) 114, 156, 160, 164, 267
Private *cabinet intérieur* of the Dauphine 168, 171, 173
Proust, Marcel 23
Provence, Comtesse de (Marie Joséphine de Savoie) 24, 89, 166
Puységur, Marquis de (Armand Marie Jacques de Chastenet) 151

Q

Queen's Bedchamber 51, 53, 55, 56, 148, 272, 275
Queen's Hamlet (*Hameau de la Reine*) 302, 306, 310, 312
Queen's Library 132, 136, 140
Queen's Private Apartment (*Petit Appartement*) 148, 151
Queen's Staircase 24, 31, 183
Queen's Suite (*Grand Appartement*) 51, 59, 124
Queen's Theater 297, 298

R

Return from the Hunt dining room 94
Riesener, Jean Henri 102, 131
Risen Burgh, Bernard Van 173
Roche, metal sculptor 204
Rousseau, brothers 92, 93, 126, 142
Royal Chapel 60, 68, 75, 77, 85, 258
Royal Opera 198, 200, 211
Royal Tribune (or gallery) 42, 60, 65, 75, 77

S

Saint-Simon, Duke of (Louis de Rouvroy) 8, 39, 40, 65, 86, 89, 220, 246, 251
Sartine, Marquis de 151
Savoy, Charles Emmanuel de 140
Schnetz, Victor 192
Schwerdfeger, Ferdinand 53
Sedaine, Michel Jean 298

Ségur, Marquis de 151
Sené, Jean Baptiste Claude 268
Slodtz, brothers 110
Sofa Room (*Cabinet de la Méridienne*) 124, 142, 145
Stags Court 94
Staircase of the Ambassadors 24, 31, 32
Staircase of the Dupes 26
Staircase of Provence 24

T

Taupin, Pierre 73
Tessé, Marquise de (Adrienne Catherine) 168
Thomire, Pierre Philippe 53, 268
Throne Room 35
Tuby, Jean Baptiste 214

U

Urban II, Pope 192

V

Valéry, Paul 211
Vatout, Jean 178
Verberckt, Jacques 36, 101, 114, 164
Vernet, Horace 178
Vernet, Louis 204
Veronese, Paolo 36
Vigée-Lebrun, Élisabeth 126, 151, 268
Villequier, Duc de (Louis-Alexandre d'Aumont) 160

W

Wailly, Charles de 204
War Room 43, 44
Werner, Jean Jacques 258
Windsor, Duchess of (Wallis Simpson) 164
Winterhalter, François Xavier 176